T0312014

Cambridge Elements ≡

Elements in the Philosophy of Science
edited by
Jacob Stegenga
University of Cambridge

DUHEM AND HOLISM

Milena Ivanova
University of Cambridge

CAMBRIDGE
UNIVERSITY PRESS

CAMBRIDGE
UNIVERSITY PRESS

University Printing House, Cambridge CB2 8BS, United Kingdom

One Liberty Plaza, 20th Floor, New York, NY 10006, USA

477 Williamstown Road, Port Melbourne, VIC 3207, Australia

314–321, 3rd Floor, Plot 3, Splendor Forum, Jasola District Centre, New Delhi – 110025, India

103 Penang Road, #05–06/07, Visioncrest Commercial, Singapore 238467

Cambridge University Press is part of the University of Cambridge.

It furthers the University's mission by disseminating knowledge in the pursuit of education, learning, and research at the highest international levels of excellence.

www.cambridge.org
Information on this title: www.cambridge.org/9781009001335
DOI: 10.1017/9781009004657

© Milena Ivanova 2021

First published 2021

A catalogue record for this publication is available from the British Library.

ISBN 978-1-009-00133-5 Paperback
ISSN 2517-7273 (online)
ISSN 2517-7265 (print)

Duhem and Holism

Elements in the Philosophy of Science

DOI: 10.1017/9781009004657
First published online: July 2021

Milena Ivanova
University of Cambridge
Author for correspondence: Milena Ivanova, mail@milenaivanova.co.uk

Abstract: The holistic thesis developed by Pierre Duhem challenges the idea that our evidence can conclusively falsify a theory. Given that no scientific theory is tested in isolation, a negative experiment can always be attributed to components other than the theory we test – to auxiliary hypotheses and background assumptions. How do scientists decide whether the experimental result undermines the theory or points at an error in the underlying assumptions? Duhem argues that we cannot offer a rule that directs when scientists should employ a radical or conservative strategy in light of a negative result, and ultimately they will appeal to their intuition. More recently philosophers have offered a number of strategies of how to locate error and justify the abandonment of a theory or an auxiliary hypothesis. This Element analyses Duhem's response to holism and subsequent accounts of how the problem can be resolved.

Keywords: theory, holism, confirmation, evidence, experiment

ISBNs: 9781009001335 (PB), 9781009004657 (OC)
ISSNs: 2517-7273 (online), 2517-7265 (print)

Contents

1 Introduction

In the 1940s the Bulgarian-born astronomer Fritz Zwicky, based at the California Institute of Technology, observed an anomalous behaviour of luminous matter; the rotational velocities of galaxies at the edge of the Coma Cluster exceeded substantially those entailed by our current theory of gravity. In the late 1960s an American astrophysicist based at the Carnegie Institute of Science, Vera Rubin, observed that stars on the periphery of a galaxy cluster orbit at similar speeds to those closer to the centre of the galaxy. These observations were not in agreement with the predictions of our theory of gravity, the general theory of relativity, so what did they entail? Was there an error in the way we made the predictions, perhaps an auxiliary hypothesis that needed modifying, or were these observations telling us our theory of gravity is false? Currently, while for some the observations point the finger at the theory, most of the community thinks some modifications to the auxiliary assumptions can accommodate these observations without questioning our central and well-established theoretical commitments.

This is the nature of holistic theory testing; our theories are never subjected to testing in isolation, but together with a whole group of assumptions and background conditions. Whether the negative result from our observations or experiments undermines the theory or points at a problem with the assumptions is not a question that can be settled by deductive reasoning. So how are scientists to proceed? In the case of the rotational speeds of galaxies that call into question our theory of gravity, many have chosen to follow what Pierre Duhem would claim is a timid or conservative path to accommodating the evidence. They have chosen to adjust the auxiliary assumptions by the postulation of dark matter that compensates for the mass required for the observed velocities that are in accord with the predictions of our theory of gravity. However, while this move was proposed in the 1970s, neither experiments designed to detect such matter nor our large particle accelerators have succeeded in detecting dark matter. A more radical or bold move, again to use Duhem's terms, was proposed by Mordehai Milgrom in 1983. This move involves substantially modifying our theory of gravity. Which move is to be preferred, how do we decide which move to follow, and how do scientists reach consensus on such a matter?

The problem of holism calls into question our ability to learn from experience. Since the time of Francis Bacon, confidence in scientific hypotheses was granted via observation and experimentation. Our ability to explore nature by setting out experiments in which we can test whether the predictions of a theory obtain has been the established method for theory confirmation. Bacon argues that experiments give us privileged access to nature. If we form a theory about a particular domain, an experiment testing the theory can either confirm it or falsify it, depending on whether the expected outcome obtains or does not. In his *Conjectures and Refutations* Karl Popper argues that the sole aim of science is to refute scientific hypotheses, and the very possibility of refutation is what grants science its status. For Popper the problem with pseudoscientific hypotheses – hypotheses that claim to be scientific or that imitate genuine science but do not share properties of what we regard as genuinely scientific theories – is exactly their ability to resist refutation. Scientific hypotheses, on the other hand, are specific enough to be refuted by scientific experimentation and observation. Popper's sentiments about falsification were in opposition to the logical positivist agenda that posited the criterion of verificationism. The idea behind this criterion is that scientific statements are empirically verifiable: our experience can confirm them. On the other hand, metaphysical hypotheses are problematic exactly because they are not subject to testing and potential confirmation by experience. Both Popper's and the positivists' theses place a significant importance on our empirical observations and experiments. Whether we look to verify or falsify our hypotheses, we rely on the idea that an experiment can conclusively produce an outcome that we can then take to either support or refute the theory we wish to test.

Pierre Duhem (1861–1916), a professor of theoretical physics in Bordeaux, significantly challenges this idea about scientific experimentation. For Duhem a negative experimental result cannot by itself falsify the hypothesis being tested, because a conjunction of hypotheses were involved in the predicted experimental result. While the experiment condemns the conjunction of the whole body of beliefs, it does not isolate where the error lies. Duhem and others after him have sought to address the question of how to isolate the problematic hypothesis. For Duhem neither the experiment itself nor the deductive reasoning we have followed provides the resources to help us solve this problem. The reason for this is that all the experimental result has told us is that there is an error within the entire set of hypotheses assumed during the testing. But the negative result is insufficient to isolate the error. It could be that the theory is false. Alternatively, one of the assumptions we used to derive the prediction or to construct and perform the experiment could be at fault for the negative observation. By its very nature an empirical finding cannot tell us where the error is, nor can it guide our decision whether to discard the theory or seek to find a faulty assumption made during the experimental set-up.

This Element investigates the origin of the holistic nature of theory testing in the work of Duhem and how his concerns about scientific practice influence the implications he draws from this problem and the solutions he offers. We examine the original formulation of Duhem's holism, in the context of his own philosophical stances, and what it implies for confirmation and theory choice. Section 2 focuses on articulating what Duhem took to be the aim of science, whether it is to find truths about the unobservable world or simply to offer us convenient tools with which we can make predictions about observable phenomena. We concentrate on the important distinction Duhem draws between two aims of science: (1) to *represent* rather than to *explain* phenomena; and (2) to offer a 'natural classification' of phenomena, his arguments for which have often been taken to be in tension with his arguments in favour of instrumentalism about science. This discussion situates the holistic argument within Duhem's views on what kind of knowledge science can afford and how science makes progress in light of the problem of holism. After outlining these arguments I turn to Duhem's articulation of the holistic nature of theory testing, as well as its methodological and epistemological implications.

Duhem argues that if a negative outcome from experiment obtains, one could still save the theory from refutation by adjusting the auxiliary hypotheses, or one could simply construct a new theory. Because one could follow two different ways of accommodating the experimental result, one could in principle end up with two theories that are equally well supported by the evidence, yet make different claims about the world. This is how Duhem arrives at the problem of underdetermination of theory by the data. In Section 3 I turn to the problem of underdetermination, which Duhem sees as a consequence of the holistic thesis, and the epistemological significance of this problem. I discuss Duhem's argument that the virtues of a theory cannot conclusively privilege a theory over its empirically equivalent rivals, and evaluate his highly contentious notion of *good sense*. I assess Duhem's argument that scientists' intuitions, rather than strict logical rules, guide decisions as to whether to reject a theory in light of the evidence or to keep it and modify other assumptions, and I evaluate the success of Duhem's concept of good sense as well as recent readings of it.

While Duhem's resolution to the problem of holistic theory testing was to turn to the scientists themselves and their virtues, contemporary philosophers responding to Duhem's challenge from holism have adopted a number of different strategies. The main aim has been to offer an account that gives us ways to locate blame, a method or set of rules that can direct our decisions as to which hypothesis in the body subjected to testing was faulty. Section 4 examines such contemporary solutions to holism. Specifically, I focus on four proposals for resolution of holism: Jon Dorling's Bayesian solution, Lindley Darden's diagnostic solution, Debora Mayo's error-statistical solution and Marcel Weber's solution using inference to the best explanation. I discuss the advantages and shortcomings of these solutions and ultimately analyse to what extent they have advanced Duhem's own intuitions about what a solution to the holistic problem can look like, arguing that Mayo and Darden's solutions preserve some of the lessons we learn from Duhem and together offer the most promising tools for the resolution of the problem.

2 Scientific Aims, Methods and the Holistic Nature of Theory Testing

In this section we examine Duhem's idea on the aim of scientific theories, drawing on his distinction between representation and explanation and the argument that science aims to classify, rather than explain, the observable phenomena. We then turn to the hypothetico-deductive method and the holistic nature of confirmation.

2.1 The Aim of Science: Explanation or Representation?

Duhem starts *The Aim and Structure of Physical Theories* with the question of what we should take as the aim of our physical theories: do they aim to classify and coordinate experimental observations into a coherent theoretical system, or do they aim to offer us the truth about the unobservable reality? Science, Duhem claims, offers us a classification of experimental laws, laws we have arrived at by generalisations from observation. Duhem draws a line between scientific processes and objects that we can observe and detect with the unaided senses and the theoretical entities and processes that we postulate via our theories but cannot access directly. We can achieve knowledge of the former via the scientific method, but our theories can never be taken to offer us the true description of the world, or the 'realities', beyond our senses. The distinction between observable and unobservable entities and processes is crucial in Duhem's position. When science employs observable entities and processes it is involved in a process of representation – classifying these processes with other similar processes and then making predictions. But once it goes beyond this realm into the domain of the unobservable, science loses its status and wanders into the realm of metaphysics.

The distinction between unobservable and observable entities is central to traditional anti-realist positions, such as logical positivism, instrumentalism and contemporary forms of empiricism, such as constructive empiricism, since these positions involve different epistemic attitudes towards observable entities and unobservable ones. Grover Maxwell (1962) has challenged this distinction on the grounds that there does not seem to be a non-arbitrary way of distinguishing what entity is observed directly and what constitutes indirect observation. At what point exactly, Maxwell asks, as we move from seeing an entity with the direct sense through lenses, binoculars, low-power microscope and high-power microscope, does an entity become not directly observable? For Maxwell, since there is no sharp line to be drawn here, the distinction falls apart and we should treat all entities as observable. For Bas van Fraassen (1980), however, Maxwell's argument shows that 'observable' is a vague term; while there are clear-cut cases in which this term applies, there are also boundary cases where it is indeterminate whether the term applies, as is the case with terms like 'mountain' and 'bald'. Van Fraassen concludes that the distinction can still be successfully utilised in most cases to guide our epistemic attitudes. This distinction plays an important role in Duhem's epistemic attitude, and his position comes close to what is sometimes referred to as eliminative instrumentalism.

Duhem argues that science can be practised successfully without aiming to address the question of whether observable phenomena have unobservable causes and seeking to identify them. The goal of science is to construct theories that summarise and classify experimental laws, not go beyond the observable phenomena. Central to this argument is the distinction between representation and explanation. Duhem argues that when we attempt to explain, we go beyond the realm of our observations, so we wander off from the domain of science into the domain of metaphysics. Explanations, because they look for causes or essences, in a sense make science less scientific. We should, for Duhem, not subordinate science to metaphysics, and thus should not wander into the territory of the unobservable. When we explain, we 'strip reality of the appearances covering it like a veil, in order to see the bare reality itself' (Duhem 1954 [1906], 7). But science is not in the business of searching for 'essences'; it is successful without needing to presuppose knowledge of a distinct reality underneath the phenomena and processes we observe. Duhem claims that were we to regard physical theories as explanations of experimental laws, then we must presuppose that 'under the sensible appearances, which are revealed in our perceptions, there is a distinct reality from these appearances' (9). But the question of whether such a reality exists, and the question of what its 'nature' is, is not something that can be established by experimental science. Science does not aim to explain the phenomena because 'it cannot render accessible to the senses the reality it proclaims as residing underneath those appearances' (8). Rather, science deals with the observable reality only and aims to clarify it in an economical manner.

For Duhem a physical theory is 'a system of mathematical propositions, deduced from a small number of principles, which aim to represent as simply, as completely, and as exactly as possible a set of experimental laws' (19). Experimental laws are generalisations of observations that the experimental physicist carefully coordinates and that the theoretical physicist then uses in the construction of the theory. Duhem sees the aim of science as providing an empirically adequate description of observable phenomena, without claiming to offer a true description of the world in itself, the world that we assume exists behind the phenomena we observe.

His notorious opposition to the atomic hypothesis and his refusal to accept the accumulating evidence in its favour is grounded in arguments concerning the nature of science and its aims. His view had strong implications for what he took to constitute genuine evidence. For instance, he was never convinced by the experimental results obtained by Jean Perrin, who provided thirteen distinct ways to calculate the number of molecules in a mole. Even after these results, which convinced many of his contemporaries to accept the atomic hypothesis, Duhem continued his opposition to atomism and defended an alternative research programme, that of energetics, the method of which he saw as more closely aligned with the method the scientific community should follow. The theory of energetics, for Duhem, aimed to derive all chemical and physical phenomena from the principles of thermodynamics, and Duhem saw it as preserving the integrity of physics by not aiming to explain the phenomena but rather to derive them from first principles.[1]

2.2 Natural Classification

Central to Duhem's view on the aim of science is the concept of natural classification. One question that arises for him from an anti-realist take on the aim of science is that we should not think of scientific theories as artificial classifications of already observed facts; rather we should aim to construct theories that reflect worldly order, that are natural.

> [T]he aim of physical theory is to become a natural classification, to establish among diverse experimental laws a logical coordination serving as a sort of image and reflection of the true order according to which the realities escaping us are organised. (Duhem 1954 [1906], 31)

Duhem gives two central arguments to defend this concept, which has given rise to a lot of interpretative disputes, with many recognising that the concept of natural classification seems to be in tension with his instrumentalist tendencies (Dion 2013). We can distinguish two arguments for when a theory is approaching a natural classification: when it unexpectedly succeeds in unifying distinct sets of phenomena, and when it successfully predicts phenomena it was not designed to account for.

---

[1] Duhem's opposition to atomism has been seen as 'hostile' and 'dogmatic' by Psillos (2014). For a discussion on Duhem's stance towards atoms, see Achinstein (2007), Coko (2015), Ivanova (2015, 2017b) and van Fraassen (2009). For a recent discussion of Perrin's experiments and their reception by the scientific community, see Coko (2020), Hudson (2020) and Ivanova (2020b).

Let us first examine the argument from unification. Duhem argues that our ability to suspect a theory is a natural classification is motivated when we see successful unification in science. Classic examples of such unifications are Maxwell's theory of electromagnetism, unifying electric and magnetic phenomena, and Isaac Newton's theory of universal gravitation, unifying terrestrial and celestial phenomena. Such success stories give us grounds to suspect these theories capture something of the worldly order, although often Duhem implies that unification is simply an ideal we work towards that helps us make sense of the world. Consider the following passages:

> Why give up the ideal of a completely unified and perfectly logical theory, when the systems actually constructed have drawn closer and closer to this ideal from century to century? (Duhem 1954 [1906], 296)
> [The physicist] will affirm that underneath the observable data, the only data accessible to his method of study, are hidden realities whose essences cannot be grasped by these same methods, and that these realities are arranged in a certain order which physical science cannot directly complete. But he will note that physical theory through its successive advances tends to arrange experimental laws in an order more and more analogous to the transcendent order according to which the realities are classified, that as a result physical theory advances gradually towards its limiting form, namely, that of a natural classification, and finally that logical unity is a characteristic without which physical theory cannot claim this rank of a natural classification. (297)

In 'The Value of Physical Theory', published in the second edition of *The Aim and Structure of Physical Theory*, Duhem addresses some of his contemporaries, like Edouard LeRoy, who endorse a conventionalist view on the aim of science and believe that physical theories are instruments suited for increasing empirical knowledge and do not aim at providing true descriptions of the world. Duhem responds to their claims as follows:

> But nature protests against this judgement; it declares that there exists a universal and necessary truth, and that physical theory through the steady progress which extends it continually while rendering it still more unified gives us from day to day a more perfect insight into this truth, so that it constitutes a veritable philosophy of the universe. (332–3)

In his historical book *To Save the Phenomena: An Essay on the Idea of Physical Theory from Plato to Galileo* Duhem further discusses how unification relates to our confidence in a theory being a natural classification. Duhem juxtaposes Kepler and Galileo, who took their theories to describe the real nature of planetary motion, against Osiander and Bellarmine, who took an instrumentalist attitude towards the astronomical models, claiming they aim to merely 'save the phenomena'. He notes the unsigned preface to Copernicus' *On the Revolutions of the Celestial Spheres*, written by Andreas Osiander, which expresses beautifully the instrumentalist thesis:[2]

> The astronomer's job consists of the following: to gather together the history of the celestial movements by means of painstakingly and skillfully made observations, and then – since he cannot by any line of reasoning reach the true causes of these movements – to think up or construct whatever hypotheses he pleases such that, on their assumption, the self-same movements, past and future both, can be calculated by means of the principle of geometry. . . . It is not necessary that these hypotheses be true. They need not even be likely. This one thing suffices, that the calculations to which they lead agree with the result of observation. (Quoted in Duhem 1969 [1908], 66)

While Duhem agrees with this stance towards science, he thinks that the lesson we learn from the historical development in astronomy is that we need to demand theories that achieve unification:

> Despite Kepler and Galileo, we believe today, with Osiander and Bellarmine, that the hypotheses of physics are mere mathematical contrivances devised for the purpose of saving the phenomena. But thanks to Kepler and Galileo, we now require that they save all of the phenomena of the inanimate universe together. (117)

The question here is, of course, how we should interpret this argument for unification. Is unification merely a regulative ideal we should aim for, or does it give us ground to think the success of our theories to unify distinct sets of phenomena justifies a realist position? I return to this question after examining Duhem's second argument for natural classification.

The second argument for natural classification is motivated by the ability of our theories to make novel predictions. A significant number of contemporary scientific realists take the strength of their position to derive from explaining how theories achieve the prediction of novel facts – facts the theories were not designed to account for. Novel predictions are fascinating, and the history of science gives us plenty of examples of such achievements. Newton's theory led to the prediction of Neptune, observed after the theory predicted its position in the heavenly skies. Mendeleev's periodic table entailed the existence of three previously unknown elements: scandium, germanium and gallium. The standard model entailed the existence of the Higgs boson. Fresnel's theory of light predicted the white spot effect that appears at the centre of an opaque disk. Einstein's theory of general relativity predicted the bending of light rays near massive bodies. The scientific

---

[2] It is worth noting that the preface did not express Copernicus' own attitude towards the theory, which was very much a realist one.

realist reasons in the following way: unless these theories are at least approximately true, how else could we explain such successes?

Realists claim that a theory's truth gives the best explanation for such success.[3] At the centre of this thesis is the assumption about the epistemic asymmetry between prediction and accommodation, the idea that predicting novel facts offers a much stronger support of the theory than the mere accommodation of known facts. We can think about a novel prediction in light of the following questions. Was the phenomenon observed prior to the theory that entailed it (temporal novelty)? Was it known to the scientists who constructed the theory that entailed it (epistemic novelty)? Was it used in the construction of the theory (use novelty)? The difficulty facing realists is to justify why they take such an asymmetric treatment between accommodation of facts and their prediction, and ultimately whether many of the historical examples in use by the realists are actually cases of accommodation, as Eric Barnes' (2008) detailed study of predictivism illustrates.

The question of interest here is the significance of novel predictions for Duhem's argument for natural classification. We are interested in whether Duhem takes novel predictions to pull us towards a more realist stance, or whether he sees instrumentalism as unchallenged in light of these cases. To return to his concept of natural classification, in the subsection on 'Theory Anticipating Experiment' of the first chapter in the *Aim and Structure of Physical Theory*, Duhem claims that:

> There is one circumstance which allows with particular clarity your belief in the natural character of a theoretical classification; this circumstance is present when we ask of a theory that it tells us the results of an experiment before it has occurred, when we give it the bold injunction 'Be a prophet for us.' (Duhem 1954 [1906], 27)

Particularly interesting is the following passage, where Duhem discusses the confidence novel predictions allow:

> [T]he more complete [a physical theory] becomes, the more we apprehend that the logical order in which theory orders experimental laws is the reflection of an ontological order, the more we suspect that the relations it establishes among the data of observation correspond to real relations among things and the more we feel that theory tends to be a natural classification. (26)

---

[3] The 'no miracles' argument is defended by Boyd (1983) and Putnam (1975), who claim that novel predictions serve as the ultimate argument for realism. van Fraassen (1980), on the other hand, thinks we should take novelty as a fitness criterion for our theories. For a detailed discussion of scientific realism and the role of the 'no miracles' argument for its success, see Chang (forthcoming).

Duhem also discusses the idea of a 'perfect theory', which will be a complete representation of all processes and entities taking place in the observable and unobservable realms. He claims that such a theory is impossible to reach via the scientific method, an idea that he thought allows space for his Catholic faith. All we can hope to achieve with the resources of science is an 'imperfect theory', a theory that at the ideal end of science could reveal relations between observable phenomena.

> [W]e do not possess this perfect theory, and mankind will never possess it; what we possess and what mankind will always possess is an imperfect and provisional theory, which by its innumerable groupings, hesitations and repentances proceeds slowly toward that ideal form which would be a natural classification. (302)

One question that emerges here is whether the concept of natural classification should be seen as an argument against instrumentalism. Some philosophers certainly take this lesson from the arguments for natural classification. Andrew Lugg (1990) and Stathis Psillos (1999) read the concept of natural classification as a defence of convergent scientific realism in contrast to instrumentalism. The idea here is that we cannot explain how scientific theories are able to act as 'prophets' and predict novel facts and also unify diverse sets of phenomena into a single framework, unless we claim the theory is approximately true. The truth here is explanatory, posited to account for scientific success.

Other philosophers think Duhem is searching for a way to reconcile both the scientific realist and instrumentalist implications of his arguments. Ernan McMullin (1990) takes Duhem's concept of natural classification to take a middle ground position between scientific realism and instrumentalism. A selective realist interpretation has also been proposed by John Worrall (1996 [1989]), Barry Gower (2000) and Milena Ivanova (2010, 2015), reading the concept for natural classification as advancing a form of structural realism.[4] According to this reading, Duhem thinks we cannot learn about the 'things' or 'essences' in the unobservable realm, but the successful theories that classify phenomena in a natural way reveal the structure of the unobservable reality. The interpretation appeals to the following claim Duhem made when discussing the concept of natural classification, the empirically successful theory that makes novel predictions and unifications and 'expresses profound and real relations

---

[4] The term 'structural realism' was introduced by Maxwell (1962), referring to the empiricist view developed by Bertrand Russell in *The Analysis of Matter* (1927). As a thesis motivated by the problem of theory change, structural realism was developed by Worrall, motivated by arguments developed by Poincaré (1902, 1913) and Duhem. The idea behind structural realism is to balance two different arguments motivated by the history of science: the argument from theory change and the 'no miracles' argument.

among things' (Duhem 1954 [1906], 28). One interesting question to consider here is why we should take the logical order Duhem takes to be found in our theories to reflect an ontological order. Furthermore, whereas Duhem seems to express a structuralist sentiment, the idea remains rather undeveloped in his writing, contrary to his contemporary Henri Poincaré, who develops the thesis in more depth and illustrates how we can identify the structural content of a theory and its preservation in theory change with the famous example of the transition from Fresnel to Maxwell's theory of light.

There is also a question of whether Duhem indeed committed to such a middle ground view. Beyond being a motivator for doing science, do we have an argument for why we should take natural classification to reflect the structure of the unobservable world? Duhem's language is rather weak, arguing that when a theory makes unexpected predictions or unifications, we 'feel' or 'suspect' our theory reflects worldly order, and often his language even sounds like a warning rather than a statement of confidence, when he tells us we 'apprehend' that the theory is indeed a natural classification. Whether we should read this as an argument for fallibilism and an expression of caution about committing to the theory's success, or whether this is simply an admission that realism is only justifiable as a motivation rather than a stance towards our theories, is a matter of dispute (Ivanova (2010, 2015).

Karen Darling (2003) and Sindhuja Bhakthavatsalam (2015), for instance, take the language Duhem uses to express his conviction that a theory is a natural classification to be best accounted for by regarding his thesis as 'motivational realism'. According to this view, Duhem is aiming to explain scientific practice rather than to offer an explanation for the success of science and argue for the approximate truth of theories. While the latter readings of Duhem's view were developed as an alternative to the selective realism interpretation, I do not see them as in conflict but rather as complementary, something Bhakthavatsalam (2015) notes as well, despite defending the latter reading over the former.

I also want to note that despite being careful about the nature of our conviction that a theory is approaching a natural classification, claiming it is a 'feeling' rather than a rationally established belief, Duhem also does give us ground for what would justify such a belief, when he uses the argument for theories acting as prophets. If this is right, Duhem does seem to suggest that a theory's novel predictive power gives us ground to 'place a bet' on a theory's future successes (Ivanova 2015).

Having reflected on Duhem's views on the aims of science and his concept of natural classification, let us now turn to his views on the scientific method and see how he arrives at the problem of holism in theory testing.

2.3 The Scientific Method and the Role of Experiment

To understand how Duhem reaches the holistic problem of theory testing, it is important for us to first discuss his view on scientific methodology and the role of experiment in it. Duhem is a monist about methodology, he is firmly opposed to inductivist schools, and he argues that science should follow the hypothetico-deductive method.[5] The following four steps are identified in the development and testing of a theory: '(1) the definition and measurement of physical magnitudes; (2) the selection of hypotheses; (3) the mathematical development of the theory; (4) the comparison of the theory with experiment' (1954 [1906], 21).

Duhem starts his important chapter 'Physical Theory and Experiment' with the following claim:

> The sole purpose of physical theory is to provide a representation and classification of experimental laws; the only test permitting us to judge a physical theory good or bad is the comparison between the consequences of this theory and the experimental laws it has to represent and classify. (180)

Duhem discusses Claude Bernard's argument that when testing a hypothesis, experimenters need to be detached from their own interests and preconceived ideas; they need to collect the results of the experiments as impartial judges (180–1). The scientist should not be guided by the theory they support and want to confirm; rather they need to be impartial and detached in order to evaluate how the experimental results fit with the theory they want to test. Here Duhem is appealing to the idea that we need to avoid confirmation bias, distortion of results and data for some personal gain or interest. But while he recognises the importance of objectivity, in this section he decides to draw our attention to the fact that observation and obtaining experimental results are never free from underlying assumptions. This is because our observations and reports of experimental results are always made through an underlying theory and a web of other assumptions.

It is in this chapter that Duhem develops the insightful argument about the theory laden-ness of observation. Duhem claims that in physics it is hard to isolate the hypothesis we are testing, since the very design of an experiment and the interpretation of its results involve taking many other theories and hypotheses as given. The experiment is not simply the observation of a phenomenon

---

[5] Duhem belongs to the generation of philosophers of science who aimed to identify a single method underlying all scientific activities, a pursuit seen as instrumental in defending the integrity and status of science, among other things. This monism about scientific methodology was questioned in the 1960s, but questions about scientific relativism and anarchy took the stage with the idea that there is no universal scientific method. For a detailed exploration of competing accounts of scientific methodology, and a defence of the idea that recognising the plurality of methods employed in science need not entail relativism, see Chalmers (2013).

but also its interpretation. We use theories in order to select data and interpret them. The idea that our theories shape how we interpret the sense data, leading to the idea that people can potentially 'see' different things depending on their theoretical assumptions, was later developed by Norwood Hanson (1958) and Thomas Kuhn (1962). Theory laden-ness is central to Kuhn's philosophy. According to him, observation is paradigm laden: scientists in different paradigms conceptualise and see the same world differently because their interpretive frameworks are different. Kuhn gives special attention to the Gestalt experiments in psychology where a subject can have the same sensory input but see two different images. Hanson famously argued that Tycho Brache and Johannes Kepler saw different things in the night sky, despite having the same sense experience (1958, 8).

Take a slightly different example – that of how not only our background assumptions, but also our personal and cultural biases can affect what we 'see' in phenomena. A male scientist studying reproduction, who carries traditional gender stereotypes, sees a different process unfolding under the microscope when studying reproduction from his counterparts not subscribing to such gender stereotypes. The former scientist sees a passive egg being heroically conquered by the active and dominant sperm.[6] The latter scientist sees a very different process in which the egg guides and clamps the sperm. To return to Duhem, it is important to recognise that observations in science are not 'raw descriptions of facts'; rather they are interpreted and systematised under adopted rules:

> [I]t is impossible to leave outside the laboratory door the theory that we wish to test, for without the theory it is impossible to regulate a single instrument or to interpret a single reading. . . . The chemist and the physiologist when they make use of physical instruments, e.g., the thermometer, the manometer, the calorimeter, the galvanometer, and the saccharimeter, implicitly admit the accuracy of the theories justifying the use of these pieces of apparatus as well as of the theories giving meaning to the abstract ideas of temperature, pressure, quantity of heat, intensity of current, and polarized light, by means of which the concrete indications of these instruments are translated. (1954 [1906], 183)

By using these theories and apparatuses for measurement, the scientist appeals to the physical theories that describe the measurements and laws involved in their obtainment, so they are implicitly showing 'faith in a whole group of theories' (183). So in physics, we cannot describe 'raw facts'; the very way in which we have obtained and reported the results has involved background theories and can very well also involve the very theory we want to test.

---

[6] For an insightful analysis of gender biases in theories of reproduction, see Martin (1991).

2.4 Holism in Theory Testing: The Problem

Duhem sees the problem from the holistic nature of confirmation as a problem of logical deduction – an experimental prediction is entailed not by the theory we would like to test but by a conjunction of statements. This conjunction involves the theory we would like to test, but also a whole group of other assumptions, from background assumptions to other laws involved in the function of the apparatus we are using. When our experimental result does not fit the expected outcome, by just following deductive logic we have condemned the entire conjunction; any of the disjuncts could be faulty. But our reasoning so far has told us nothing as to how to proceed and isolate the faulty hypothesis.[7] Let us follow how exactly Duhem describes the problem:

> The physicist who carries out an experiment, or gives a report of one, implicitly recognises the accuracy of a wide group of theories. (183)
> [I]f the predicted phenomenon is not produced, not only is the proposition questioned at fault, but so is the whole theoretical scaffolding used by the physicist. The only thing the experiment teaches us is that among the propositions used to predict the phenomenon and to establish whether it would be produced, there is at least one error; but where this error lies is just what it does not tell us. The physicist may declare that the error is contained in exactly the proposition he wishes to refute, but is he sure that it is not in another proposition? (185)

For Duhem this is a logical problem that leads to the problem of action: how is the scientist to act in such situations?

> [T]he physicist can never subject an isolated hypothesis to experimental test, but only a whole group of hypotheses; when the experiment is in disagreement with his predictions, what he learns is that at least one of the hypotheses constituting this group is unacceptable and ought to be modified; but the experiment does not designate which one should be changed. (187)

Duhem gives an interesting analogy here between a watchmaker trying to fix a broken watch and a doctor trying to diagnose an illness in a patient. While the former is in a position to dissect the watch into pieces and identify which of them is broken, the doctor can only guess the diagnosis by looking at the consequences of the disorder in the whole body. The physicist operates like the doctor rather than the watchmaker – physical theory is like a system that is always taken as a whole.

---

[7] Duhem's thesis and its implications are explored in Ariew (1984), Brenner (1990), Dietrich and Honenberger (2020), Grünbaum (1962), Harding (1975), Massey (2011), Mayo (1996) and Rowbottom (2010) among others.

Duhem distinguishes between experiments of application and experiments of testing. The former are simply applications of accepted theories and, in his words, their performance presents 'nothing to shock logic' (184). On the other hand, the latter are designed to test and confirm or condemn theories, and the problem of holism emerges in this context.

> To seek to separate each of the hypotheses of theoretical physics from the other assumptions on which the science rests in order to subject it in isolation to observational test is to pursue a chimera; for the realization and interpretation of no matter what experiment in physics imply adherence to a whole set of theoretical presuppositions. (199–200)

As Duhem continues this argument, the involvement of judgement and the lack of a unique prescription for action become central:

> The only experimental check in a physical theory which is not illogical consists in comparing the entire system of the physical theory with the whole group of experimental laws, and in judging whether the latter is represented by the former in a satisfactory manner. (200)

In such a situation where an experiment has condemned a whole body of propositions, scientists can respond in two ways: they can accommodate the negative result by rejecting the theory they wanted to test, taking it that the negative result indicated fault with the theory itself, or they can modify the initial conditions and background assumptions, taking it that the error must be in the way the original prediction was derived or the way the experiment was set up. Duhem calls these two 'paths' of identifying the 'source of error': (1) a radical, bold move; and (2) a conservative, timid move. While there is no logical argument that can impose action in one of the two ways, Duhem claims that in practice scientists are cautious to rush into radical move because:

> By taking the first alternative we should be obliged to destroy from top to bottom a very vast theoretical system which represents in a most satisfactory manner a very extensive and complex set of experimental laws. The second alternative, on the other hand, does not make us lose anything of the terrain already conquered by physical theory; in addition, it has succeeded in so large a number of cases that we can bank with interest on a new success. (211)

Duhem argues that in each theoretical period there are some assumptions that scientists just accept beyond dispute and are unlikely to question, so they will work first on other assumptions that might be in error. But their action in picking some hypotheses for modification over others is not grounded in 'logical necessity' (211). And while the bold path is not recommended in most situations, it is in such cases where a scientist decides to revisit the theory under test that we can make progress, since this move results in the development of new, more successful theories.

This section introduced the reader to Duhem's views on the aim of science, the relationship between science and metaphysics, the scientific method and the role of experiment in it, advocating for the theoretical laden-ness of our observations and the interpretation of experimental results. Having addressed Duhem's views on the kind of knowledge science affords us and the nature of scientific progress, we explored how Duhem arrives at the holistic problem of theory testing. As the previous section revealed, for Duhem this is a logical problem that presses us to recognise the role of judgement in scientific decision-making. He identifies two moves available to the scientist in situations where the experiment does not agree with our prediction, and we see that there are no logical rules to settle which move is to be made in a particular case. In the next section, I explore in depth what this argument implies about decision-making and how Duhem proposes to solve the problem of holism.

3 Holism, Underdetermination and Good Sense

3.1 The Problem of Underdetermination of Theory by the Evidence

The holistic nature of theory testing illustrates that we cannot conclusively disconfirm a theory by obtaining a negative experimental result. In this section we explore the implications Duhem sees from this thesis. For Duhem what we need to determine is how to proceed when our experimental results do not agree with the predictions we made. Do we abandon the theory we are testing, or do we try to locate the problem in one of the auxiliary assumptions used in the prediction of the result? These two paths available to the scientist are identified as 'bold' and 'timid'. The former path is rather radical – this is where we focus on modifying or abandoning the theory – while the latter path is concentrated on keeping our central commitments intact by adjusting auxiliary hypotheses involved in the testing. Such can be assumptions about the initial and boundary conditions involved in the derivations of the predictions or assumptions and laws governing the operation of the apparatus we are using to obtain the result. At the time when the scientist is faced with this choice, they are not guided by any rules or methods; they need to use their judgement to decide how to accommodate the evidence. In the introduction I discussed a contemporary case in astrophysics where the observations of rotational speeds of galaxies violate our current theories of gravity, both the Newtonian theory of gravity and Einstein's general theory of relativity. Scientists have proposed different ways to accommodate this negative result. The timid move involves the postulation of dark matter while the bolder move involves modifying our theory of gravity.

A further case to illustrate these alternative paths of pursuit concerns the Newtonian theory of gravity and some of the anomalies it faced.

A persistent anomaly for Newtonian mechanics was the perturbed motion of Uranus' orbit. The observed orbit often deviated significantly from the orbit predicted by the theory (Kollerstrom 2006). In 1846 Urbain Le Verrier proposed the existence of the planet Neptune. In light of the disagreement between the theory's prediction and the observations, Le Verrier decided to adjust the auxiliaries rather than question the theory. The postulation of Neptune was an example of adjusting other hypotheses and then accommodating the problematic observation. This was a successful move – within a year two astronomers had independently of each other observed the planet: Johann Galle at the Berlin Observatory and John Couch Adams at the University of Cambridge.

Assuming the theory is right and there must be something faulty with the auxiliary assumptions – in our case a planet whose motion perturbs that of Uranus and is therefore responsible for its irregular motion – paid off. But this kind of adjustment does not always lead to success, as Duhem argues. Take the same scientist, Le Verrier, who employed this exact move a few years later when trying to accommodate the anomalous advance of the perihelion of Mercury by proposing that the planet's movement was similarly being perturbed by a hitherto unknown planet, which he named Vulcan. Despite attempts to detect the planet, the anomaly was accommodated with the advancement of the theory of relativity. The former is clearly a timid move while the latter is a bold move, each with its own successes and failures. Duhem's point is that neither our logical rules nor our experience can dictate which move we should employ, and the success of each strategy can be judged only once further developments in science have taken place and additional evidence has spoken in favour of one of the strategies.

The important part of Duhem's argument so far is that which of these moves is right is ultimately not a question we can answer until further empirical evidence is available to support one of the theories. But when faced with this choice, scientists need to use something beyond the rules of logic and experience. And because the evidence can be accounted for by these two distinct moves, by either adjusting the background assumptions or substantially modifying the theory or developing a new one, we could also arrive at two distinct theories that accommodate the available evidence. This is how Duhem arrives at the problem of underdetermination: two theories can agree with all the available evidence we have but disagree substantially as to what the world is like. So how do we decide which theory to adopt? Since the theories agree with the current evidence, our choice cannot be driven by empirical data, so what are the options?

Contemporary philosophers have distinguished a number of ways to think about the problem of underdetermination and its significance, and it is useful here to employ some modern distinctions in order to understand Duhem's position. We can discern between local, transient or weak underdetermination, and global underdetermination. The former occurs at the level of local theories, theories applicable to a specific domain (such as a theory of gravity, of electromagnetism, etc.), and the underdetermination between such theories is of a weak nature because further evidence can come along to resolve it, by supporting one of the two theories that can accommodate it.

Consider, for instance, the wave and particle theories of light – two local theories whose domain is optical phenomena – that were weakly underdetermined. The wave theory of light originated in Aristotle's claim that light is a disturbance that occurs in the air; Descartes developed this idea during the 1630s, claiming that light is a wave-like disturbance that occurs in a medium he called the 'plenum' (Achinstein 1991). The particle theory of light originated in Democritus, according to whom everything in the universe is composed of 'atoms' – indivisible building blocks of matter.

During the 1680s Newton advanced the corpuscular theory of light, according to which reflection is a particle-like behaviour because only particles could travel in straight lines. Refraction was explained by the acceleration of particles as they enter denser mediums. However, Robert Hooke, Christian Huygens and Augustin-Jean Fresnel formalised the wave theory of light and showed that it can explain refraction as a propagation of light waves in a medium by presupposing that light travels at different speeds in different mediums (for example, light travels faster in air than in water). After the discovery of the phenomenon of interference by Thomas Young's double-slit experiment, the wave theory of light became predictively better than the particle theory of light. This extra prediction broke the underdetermination between the two theories.

This problem is localised in time and is transient because we usually expect further evidence to resolve it. Some philosophers think that the transient form of underdetermination is not threatening because all it tells us is that sometimes we do not have sufficient evidence to distinguish between competing theories (Hoefer and Rosenberg 1994). In its strong form, however, the problem of undetermination poses a serious worry because it takes place at the level of global theories, theories that would equally well fit the same evidence:

> The problem of underdetermination of theory by evidence is, in its most acute (and therefore most interesting) form, a problem for global theories, or total science: If there can be two genuine, incompatible global theories that are

equally well confirmed by all possible evidence, we face an epistemic dilemma that we cannot hope to evade through the further progress of science, or extension of theory to cover new domains. (Hoefer and Rosenberg 1994, 592)[8]

Many, including Duhem himself, however, are sceptical when it comes to such strong forms of underdetermination. The reason for taking the problem of underdetermination of weak rather than strong form is because of doubt about the possibility of arriving at a global theory. Duhem argues that even if we imagine reaching a stage in science where inquiry ends, we would still not have obtained what he calls a 'perfect theory', a theory that explains all phenomena. As he reflects:

> [W]e do not possess this perfect theory, and mankind will never possess it; what we possess and what mankind will always possess is an imperfect and provisional theory, which by its innumerable groupings, hesitations and repentances proceeds slowly toward that ideal form which would be a natural classification. (Duhem 1954 [1906], 302)

Duhem's scepticism is shared by Larry Laudan and Jarrett Leplin (1991) and Yemima Ben-Menahem (2006), who argue against the possibility of strong underdetermination. Such scepticism is often also based on the observation that many times in the history of science we had thought we had reached the 'end of science' and had thus constructed a 'final' theory (or a 'theory of everything'), only to discover new phenomena down the line that call for the development of a further theory. Michael Redhead (1995) gives a nice example from the status of physics in the 1920s, when scientists expressed confidence in having uncovered all the fundamental laws of nature and speculated that it was a matter of months before physics was complete.

> There was only one sort of matter composed of corpuscles of positive and negative electricity, and only one sort of interaction, electromagnetism, aside from gravitation and that had been sorted out by Einstein in his General Theory of Relativity. (Redhead 1995, 64)

Unfortunately those who dreamt of a final theory could not have been further from it, as it took only a few years for fundamental physics to look rather different; as Redhead states, 'what looked simple in 1927 looks very messy 40 years later' (65).

---

[8] Sklar (1974) and Worrall (2009) also accept that strong underdetermination of global theories presents a serious worry, but they believe that it can be resolved by the Ramsey sentence approach, which guarantees that any two observationally equivalent theories can be shown to be structurally equivalent.

Other examples from the history of science facilitate this sceptical inference. Newtonian mechanics was considered a 'theory of everything', but it eventually became clear that it gives incorrect predictions when we consider bodies moving with a very high velocity relative to a certain frame of reference, which is more accurately described by the special theory of relativity, and it fails to account for phenomena at the subatomic level, which are described by quantum mechanics. Doubts concerning the possibility of a 'final' or 'perfect' theory restricts the scope of the underdetermination problem; for Duhem the problem is strictly localised in time and resolvable by further evidence. But the focus for Duhem is to understand what happens when making this judgement as to how to respond to the negative experimental results before we have more evidence in favour of one particular 'path'.

3.2 Non-empirical Factors in Theory Choice

With these contemporary distinctions in mind, let us return to Duhem, who takes the challenge of underdetermination to be transient, resolvable by further evidence. Despite seeing the problem as localised in time, he nevertheless takes it to present a challenge for decision-making. While holding that two theories fitting the current data are indistinguishable in light of the evidence only temporarily, he reflects on how scientists go about justifying what theory to work with in the meantime. For Duhem the question of how scientists choose which theory to adopt has both a descriptive and a normative dimension; his aim is not only to offer a description of the process scientists follow in reaching a decision, but also to offer guidance on how they should act.

Like many contemporary philosophers, Duhem thinks that in situations when the evidence is not sufficient to guide our choice between competing alternatives, we appeal to non-empirical considerations, often referred to as 'super-empirical' criteria, theory virtues or aesthetic values of the theory itself. While two theories can accommodate the same evidence, they might have very different aesthetic qualities or virtues, so the scientist will judge which theory to choose based on those factors. The list of such aesthetic criteria usually includes the theory's simplicity, unifying power, symmetry, scope, elegance and even beauty.[9] Duhem recognises the involvement of such values in the

---

[9] Often theories are praised for qualities that are of an aesthetic nature, such as beauty or elegance, and scientists report experiencing aesthetic responses to beautiful theories. Duhem himself argues that simple and convenient theories are beautiful (1954 [1906], 24). This is a complex question, since (1) it is not at all straightforward how to define exactly what constitutes an aesthetic experience, and (2) beauty is often regarded as a subjective quality, while the aspiration has been to invoke an objective measure of a theory's quality in theory choice. For a discussion of aesthetic criteria in science, see Ivanova (2017a, 2020a, 2021), Ivanova and French (2020), McAllister (1996) and Todd (2008).

scientist's choices, but he also acknowledges their contingent nature, recognising that virtues alone cannot be taken to lead to a conclusive choice:

> No doubt the physicist will choose between these logically equivalent theories, but the motives which will dictate his choice will be considerations of elegance, simplicity, and convenience, and grounds of suitability which are essentially subjective, contingent, and variable with time, with schools, and with persons. As serious as these motives may be in certain cases, they will never be of a nature that necessitates adhering to one of the two theories and rejecting the other, for only the discovery of a fact that would be represented by one of the theories, and not by the other, would result in a forced opinion. (288)

Duhem's take on the role of theoretical virtues in theory choice predates the highly important argument developed by Kuhn regarding the nature of theory choice based on theoretical virtues. In his influential (1977) paper 'Objectivity, Value Judgment, and Theory Choice' Kuhn raises the question of whether theory choice in light of theoretical virtues is possible.[10] He argues that even if we could agree on a settled list of virtues that are inter-paradigmatically accepted – something he had questioned in his classic *The Structure of Scientific Revolutions* (1962) – such an agreement cannot guarantee that scientists are going to reach a conclusive choice about which paradigm is preferable. Kuhn takes the values of accuracy, consistency, scope, simplicity and fruitfulness to be inter-paradigmatically accepted and serving as a 'shared base' for choosing between alternative theories, meaning that scientists agree on the importance of these values independently of the paradigm within which they work. But even if we can agree on such a settled list, since we could interpret the virtues in a plurality of ways and take each one of them to be more important than the rest, this process alone cannot guarantee a conclusive choice among scientists.

To illustrate Kuhn's argument, consider the dispute between Everettian quantum mechanics and Bohmian mechanics. Whether we adopt the former or the latter depends on what values we take these theories to satisfy. I might prioritise simplicity and take it that Everettian quantum mechanics is preferable, since Bohmian mechanics adds additional ('guiding') equations to the standard formulation. But one could immediately respond that I only arrived at my conclusion by prioritising simplicity over other values, and by taking

---

[10] While Kuhn centres the question about theory virtues around the question of the rationality of theory choice, a different question takes place in the realism-empiricism debate, where the question is whether such factors should influence our confidence in the theory's truth. McMullin (2009) explores the realist argument from theory virtues, and more recently Schindler (2018) has argued that the virtues of theories offer the ultimate argument for realism. Such a connection between virtues and truthlikeness has been questioned by van Fraassen (1980). See Ivanova (2020a, forthcoming) for further reflections on the significance of van Fraassen's arguments.

simplicity to mean the number of equations. Were I to prioritise continuity or unity with existing theories, I might prefer Bohmian mechanics for its preservation of determinism. And were I to understand simplicity in terms of metaphysical economy, I might again prioritise Bohmian mechanics over Everettian quantum mechanics, since the latter postulates ontologically superfluous worlds.[11] The important point Kuhn emphasises is that ultimately even if we settle on a list of values that we are going to accept inter-paradigmatically, we cannot guarantee that scientists are going to converge in their choices, since they can make very different judgements when it comes to prioritising and defining the theories' virtues. For Kuhn these values do not determine the choice of a paradigm but influence it, and the choices cannot be justified 'though the experience of scientists provides no philosophical justification for the values they deploy . . . those values are in part learned from that experience, and they evolve with it' (335).

James McAllister has further defended the variance of theoretical virtues and the role of training in his *Beauty and Revolution in Science* (1996). He sees values such as elegance, simplicity, unity and symmetry as constituting aes-thetic criteria that inform scientists' actions. McAllister's important contribu-tion is to recognise that our aesthetic judgements are subject to change, that the concept of beauty is dynamic and that a theory considered beautiful today may later lose its aesthetic status in light of changing aesthetic canons. We can illustrate the dynamicity of the concept of beauty with a variety of historical examples that show how our appreciation of different virtues can change depending on the paradigms we employ. New virtues can come about and influence our future decisions, as can be illustrated with the case of symmetry after the development of relativity theory, or mathematical elegance after Newton's revolutionary development of calculus to express physical laws. Equally some values can lose their importance when a new theory breaks away from the established aesthetic canon, as is the case with visualisation post quantum mechanics. For McAllister this shows us that our appreciation of theoretical virtues is generated by our appreciation of the empirical success of a theory, learning from our practices which virtues to trust and desire to preserve in the development of future theories.

Duhem predates the arguments for the contingency and variance of theoret-ical virtues/values, developed in depth by Kuhn and McAllister. We can extract three lessons from Duhem's discussion of theoretical virtues. First, the theoret-ical virtues are to be regarded as pragmatic, not epistemic. They might influence

---

[11] For a discussion of the virtues of the different competitors in quantum mechanics, see Cushing (1994) and Ivanova (2014).

the choice we make to adopt a theory, but the choice leads to the employment of a theory that is convenient; the virtues do not legitimise inferring that the theory is more likely to be true.[12]

Second, the list of virtues is not set in stone. They are dynamic and closely related to the training and traditions in which the scientists are embedded. For this very reason, even though they are part of theory choice, we cannot guarantee scientists will converge in their decisions when they choose alternative competitors, since they can be prioritising different virtues and interpreting them in a plurality of ways.

Third, the virtues of a theory can only influence the choice of a theory, but does not give it the same justification as empirical evidence. At best we have weaker grounds on which to prefer one theory over another, but only the discovery of new evidence that is accommodated by one theory over its rival can settle the debate and conclusively prioritise one theory over another.

Recognising the fact that theoretical virtues are insufficient in theory choice, Duhem turns to the scientists themselves. While fully appreciating that further evidence can resolve theory choice conclusively, Duhem discusses how scientists proceed when faced with negative evidence from an experiment and how we can reach consensus when the evidence is insufficient to direct whether timid or bold moves are adequate. Let us turn to his response to the problem of holism and the underdetermination problem he saw it to entail.

3.3 'Good Sense Is the Judge of Hypotheses Which Ought to Be Abandoned'

Duhem concludes his chapter on the holistic nature of theory testing with a subsection titled 'Good Sense Is the Judge of Hypotheses Which Ought to Be Abandoned'. The idea he develops here is that once we recognise that neither our experimental result nor the deductive process by which we have arrived at the prediction have the capacity to guide us in isolating where the problematic assumption is, we need to step outside logic and the experiment and look for guidance elsewhere. It is here that he introduces the faculty of good sense, an intuition that guides the experimenter in what path to follow, whether more experiments need to be done, whether the working hypothesis needs modification, or whether we should revisit the auxiliary assumptions. Good sense takes up a small part of Duhem's chapter on experimentation and

---

[12] This is in opposition to many classic and contemporary thinkers, who take there to be a connection between truth and beauty, going back to Plato, Newton, Dirac and Einstein, or who express the idea that the aesthetic values of a theory are truth indicative. For a discussion of the epistemic significance of aesthetic values, see Breitenbach (2013), Ivanova (2017a, 2020a, 2021) and Ivanova and French (2020).

the holistic nature of theory testing in *The Aim and Structure of Physical Theory*. However, he returns to elaborate further on this notion in *German Science* (1991 [1915]), where Duhem steps outside the context of experimental physics and focuses on the role of good sense in non-experimental fields, specifically mathematics and history.

While Duhem elaborates further on the application of good sense in contexts beyond experimental physics in his later book, it is noteworthy that no new properties of good sense are introduced there; he remains consistent with respect to what good sense is while expanding its area of application. It is in this book that Duhem brings the moral dimension of good sense more explicitly and discusses the importance of training and practice for the cultivation of good sense. For my analysis I follow both works to arrive at a set of properties associated with good sense before we explore the function it plays in the holistic argument for theory testing.

3.3.1 What Are the Properties of Good Sense?

The starting point in our analysis of Duhem's notion of good sense is to note that this faculty is introduced in the context of holism when deductive logic and experience are not sufficient to dictate how we should go about addressing a negative result from an experiment; in this context the scientist turns to their intuition, their good sense. Good sense offers 'motivations which do not proceed from logic and yet direct our choices' (Duhem 1954 [1906], 217). When we obtain a result that does not agree with our predictions, there is an absence of strict rules; rather scientists follow what Duhem calls 'reasons of the heart' that guide them in how to proceed: 'no absolute principle dictates this inquiry, which different physicists may conduct in very different ways without having the right to accuse one another of illogicality' (216). If we are looking for an answer from deductive logic, both the 'timid' and 'bold' paths are justifiable.

> [T]he rules of syllogistic logic are not adequate. They must be assisted by a certain sense of soundness that is one of the forms of good sense. . . . Good sense will intervene at the moment at which one realizes that the consequences of a preconceived idea are either contradicted or confirmed by the experiment. . . . What a delicate task, concerning which no precise rule can guide the mind! It is essentially a matter of insight and ingenuity! (Duhem 1991 [1915], 23–5)

In addition to being a form of non-rule-governed process, Duhem also introduces a moral dimension to the faculty of good sense. We have already noted that when faced with the choice of how to accommodate the negative result from an experiment, we can follow the 'bold' or the 'timid' path, and for Duhem what is important is that scientists remain open-minded towards the move they are not taking and do not become prejudiced towards their own decision-making or the theory at which they arrived. Their choices should not be driven by self-interest; they should act by 'leaving their interests and passions aside' (43). Duhem appeals to Claude Bernard to state that:

> [T]he sound experimental criticism of a hypothesis is subordinated to certain moral conditions; in order to estimate correctly the agreement of a physical theory with the facts, it is not enough to be a good mathematician and skillful experimenter; one must also be an impartial and faithful judge (1954 [1906], 218).

The significance of good sense and its moral dimension comes out particularly in the case of history. While in physics scientists are mostly guided by the deductive method, with situations like underdetermination requiring the employment of good sense, in the case of history, there is not a specific method that the historian follows, so the pursuit of knowledge is entirely dependent on the good sense of the historian. As a consequence, the role of the intellectual and moral qualities of the knower become particularly important:

> In the realm of every science, but more particularly in the realm of history, the pursuit of truth not only requires intellectual abilities, but also calls for moral qualities: rectitude, probity, detachment of all interests and all passions. (Duhem 1991 [1915], 43)

After introducing good sense as a cluster of intellectual and moral virtues, Duhem turns to the role of training and practice in cultivating good sense, an aspect he sees as having an important implication for scientific progress. He claims that good sense is not equally present in all scientists and scientists should actively aim to cultivate their good sense through education and training in order to promote a faster resolution to situations of underdetermination:

> [T]hese reasons of good sense do not impose themselves with the same implacable rigour that the prescriptions of logic do. There is something vague and uncertain about them; they do not reveal themselves at the same time with the same degree of clarity to all minds. (1954 [1906], 217)
>
> Since logic does not determine with strict precision the time when an inadequate hypothesis should give way to a more fruitful assumption, and since recognizing this moment belongs to good sense, physicists may hasten this judgement and increase the rapidity of scientific progress by trying consciously to make good sense within themselves more lucid and more vigilant. (218)

We have identified several aspects to good sense: (1) it is not reducible to logic, rules or an algorithmic process; (2) it is a cluster of intellectual and moral virtues and undermined by personal bias, passions and self-interest; (3) it is not equally present in all scientists and is cultivated by practice and education; (4) it is involved in situations of underdetermination where the evidence and theoretical virtues are insufficient to dictate a solution, but also in non-empirical sciences or sciences that lack a method; (5) it accelerates scientific progress.[13]

Now I want to focus on understanding the function of good sense in Duhem's argument. Duhem appeals to good sense when he wants to illustrate how situations of underdetermination have been resolved in the past, making it clear this concept is supposed to be descriptive of the history of science. When discussing the case of the emission hypothesis, Duhem illustrates how good sense can explain historical episodes where scientists faced the problem of holism and were pursuing both timid and bold paths.

> [T]his state of indecision does not last forever. The day arrives when good sense comes out so clearly in favour of one of the sides that the other gives up the struggle even though pure logic would not forbid its continuation. (218)

The example Duhem gives of such a clear win for good sense was Biot's abandonment of the emission hypothesis in favour of wave optics. For Duhem Biot's decision to abandon the hypothesis was not due to a crucial experiment confirming wave optics; after Foucault showed light travels faster in air than in water, there was more reason to take wave optics seriously and to leave the emission hypothesis. This weighing of results in favour and against a hypothesis and the right time to abandon it is what cannot be dictated by strict logical rules and is a matter of the scientist's good sense.

Duhem recognises something rather important about practice: determining at what stage we are past the point of obtaining sufficient evidence in favour of a hypothesis is not subject to an algorithmic application of rules – it requires judgement. We can further appreciate this point by recalling the example of the atomic hypothesis. We accept today that the dispute about the existence of the atom was settled by Jean Perrin's calculations of Avocadro's number, which stands for the number of molecules in a mole. What the community regarded as significant about Perrin's work was that he arrived at the same results by following thirteen different procedures. But at what stage did Perrin's experiments tip the scale towards atomism and speak in favour of abandoning energetics, the programme Duhem defended throughout his career? At what point of Perrin's work could we say the evidence is evidence enough? Why

---

[13] The list of properties and the importance of the accelerating property of good sense is developed in Ivanova and Paternotte (2013).

thirteen determinations rather than more or fewer? There is clearly no rule that prescribes when the evidence is evidence enough, and Duhem is arguing for exactly this point: scientists need to make judgements that are not a product of strict logical rules but more aligned with their intuitions, their 'feelings of the heart'. This important point is the focus of Peter Galison's (1987) book *How Experiments End*, a study of a number of experiments in physics that illuminates the employment of judgement and values the community invokes to determine when experiments should end. When we have obtained enough evidence and we are satisfied with the quality of the results, we need judgement and consensus, neither of which are arrived at by following an algorithmic process.

In addition to its descriptive purpose, with the argument for the cultivation of good sense and its role for scientific progress, Duhem makes clear the concept has a normative dimension. He argues that when scientists are trying to identify which road to pursue, the timid or the bold, it is unproductive to be biased towards one's pet theory and closed-minded with regard to alternative solutions because the presence of bias and dogmatism can be harmful for scientific progress:

> [N]othing will delay the decision which should determine a fortunate reform in a physical theory more than the vanity which makes a physicist too indulgent towards his own system and too severe towards the system of another. (1954 [1906], 218)

Because we want to accelerate scientific progress, scientists ought to train and cultivate their good sense and virtuous character. With these properties in mind we can now turn to analysing how we can understand the role and function of good sense in Duhem's holism argument.

3.3.2 Interpreting Good Sense and Its Function

Good sense is supposed to offer guidance as to when the right time has come to abandon a hypothesis or to stop modifying auxiliaries. This very property is the focus of Philippe Mongin's (2009) reading, which emphasises the importance of the temporal dimension of good sense, the idea that scientists lack good sense either when they hastily abandon a hypothesis or when they cling on to a hypothesis for too long:

> The conservative physicist becomes unbearable only when he repairs the existing theory over and over, and the radical is unpalatable only when he strikes too early. (2009, 314)

The observation that good sense can be understood as a cluster of intellectual and moral virtues has motivated reading good sense as a virtue-theoretic concept. David Stump (2007) argues that what we see in Duhem's argument is a shift in the direction of analysis, from thinking about the deductive method that leads to the problem of holism, to thinking about the traits of the scientist choosing a direction in the absence of rules. This shift in analysis is analogous to the way virtue epistemologists think about epistemic success, from thinking about the process of knowledge acquisition to thinking about the virtues of the knower themselves (Zagzebski 2003). Furthermore, we see important commonality in the virtues Duhem appeals to, including impartiality, intellectual sobriety, rectitude, probity and intellectual courage, that are very much part of the constitutive virtues of the knower according to the virtue-theoretic analysis of knowledge. Stump argues that:

> Like contemporary virtue epistemologists, Duhem also takes knowledge to be dependent on the virtues of the knower. Scientists must have intellectual and, indeed, moral virtues in order to reach scientific knowledge, especially when choosing between empirically adequate theories. (2007, 150)

And importantly, just like we cannot construct an algorithm to decide the outcome of a moral choice, for instance, we cannot rely on an algorithm to resolve theory choice.

> Despite his holism and his famous thesis that it is always possible to save a scientific theory from refutation by empirical evidence, Duhem thinks that scientists are able to weigh evidence and to make decisions, and that the decisions they make depend on the intellectual and moral virtues of the scientist as a cognitive agent (151).
>
> In Duhem's account of scientific theory choice, there is openness, since strict rules do not apply, but also objectivity. The source of this objectivity is the epistemic agent – the scientist who acts as an impartial judge and makes the final decision (155).

Since Stump's reconstruction of good sense, seen as a cluster of intellectual and moral traits that guide scientists' choices without appeals to rules, there has been some debate on the specifics. What kind of virtue epistemology has Duhem defended? What is the function of good sense? And who instantiates it? There is some divergence in the literature on how these questions are to be addressed. However, there is also agreement that Duhem has switched the order of analysis, that good sense is constituted by virtues that are desirable and that should be cultivated in scientists, and that good sense has both descriptive and prescriptive dimensions: it is used to explain how scientists arrive at consensus and is further used to direct scientists on how to act. Starting with the question of what kind of virtue epistemology is more helpfully employed as a reading of Duhem's argument, Ian James Kidd (2011) proposes that we see Duhem's notion as a responsibilist virtue-theoretic concept, since Duhem places emphasis on the moral character and set of virtues employed by agents, rather than on the process of belief formation. On the other hand, Abrol Fairweather (2012) suggests that the notion is compatible with both reliablist and responsibilist virtue epistemology.[14] One problem these proposals have to address is why moral character is instrumental for resolving Duhem's problem and if it is in itself sufficient, something that has been the focus of the social reconstruction of good sense defended in Milena Ivanova and Cedric Paternotte (2013).

Another question regards the function of good sense: does it suffice to resolve disagreement and divergence of opinions in the community? For instance, in Ivanova (2010) I express a worry that good sense might not have the resources to conclusively justify preference of one theory over another because Duhem himself admits that only new evidence that is later obtained and supports one of the hypotheses over its rival can decisively justify the choice. If this is right, the success of good sense seems to be judged retrospectively, after the competitor is supported by new evidence.

To resolve this worry, Fairweather (2011) proposes a hybrid account of good sense that preserves the insight of Stump's reading of good sense but accommodates the problem that good sense cannot bolster epistemic standing. According to the hybrid account, the importance of good sense is that it can isolate a competitor, which theory we should adopt, but it cannot confer epistemic standing to the chosen theory, so new evidence is needed to bolster epistemic support. On this account, good sense can confer uniqueness in theory choice but cannot provide epistemic standing to a chosen theory, and the role of good sense is limited to a very specific application: resolving underdetermination.

Finally, the question of who instantiates good sense is the subject of the account, developed in Ivanova and Paternotte's (2013), where good sense is seen from the perspective of social epistemology. According to this account, we can understand good sense as a faculty that operates at the social level by ensuring that scientists, by leaving aside their bias, dogmatism and self-interest, can faster arrive at a consensus as to which move, timid or bold, they will focus. Seen as operating at the social level, good sense ensures that scientists do not stick to unproductive ideas for too long, leading the community to reach consensus faster. This account overcomes the worry of how we settle who has good sense and its retrospective justification and, importantly, it accommodates the accelerating property of good sense.

This account, however, as is the case with the accounts that follow Stump's reading of good sense, does deviate from Duhem's own insights. The focus of

---

[14] More recently Bhakthavatsalam (2017) has defended a responsibilist reading.

this account is no longer to address the question of what Duhem meant by the concept of good sense, but rather to address how this notion can be understood to work so it can be seen to deliver a solution to Duhem's problem. Duhem is clear that good sense is to be analysed as a property of individuals and does not direct us to see science from a social angle.

The idea behind the social account is that scientists will start with different preconceived ideas on the expected evidence, support different theories and vary with respect to how they interpret super-empirical criteria, so their views are bound to vary as well. We can see good sense as a process of smoothing such variance. On this reading, moral and epistemic vices are problematic because they are likely to increase the variance in the scientific community.

Here, however, it is important to discuss several potential problems that stem from the literature on social epistemology that concerns the role of diversity and uniformity for scientific progress. Much of the literature in social epistemology over the past decades has been dedicated to studying the positive effects of diversity for the achievement of epistemic aims. Taking into consideration the work of Philip Kitcher (1993) and Michael Strevens (2003), for instance, who defend the significance of distribution of cognitive labour and diversity in science, it could be argued that bias and dogmatism can have beneficial effects on the diversification of the community's efforts.[15]

Furthermore, results from formal social epistemology can be seen to suggest that maverick behaviour, which can exemplify bias and dogmatism towards one's own ideas, can be good for the epistemic success of the group if sufficient numbers of scientists do not exemplify this behaviour. According to the accounts provided by Michael Weisberg and Ryan Muldoon (2009) and Kevin Zollman (2010), the most optimal community of scientists includes a small number of 'maverick' scientists and a large number of 'followers'. Some of these models suggest that biased individuals can promote epistemic diversity in the community, since their beliefs could be extreme or resistant to certain evidence.

Zollman notes a number of factors that could serve for scientists to develop extreme prior beliefs and dogmatic behaviour in the community, such as

---

[15] It is interesting to consider the broader implications from these studies for our understanding of epistemic vice. We accept that epistemic and moral vices are bad, and epistemic vice can lead to harm, undermine epistemic aims and perpetuate epistemic and other forms of oppression, as has been argued by Fricker (2007) and further explored in several contributions in Pohlhaus and Kidd (2017), and Kidd, Battaly and Cassam (2020). Some questions that deserve further exploration are whether the latter works direct us towards rejection of the findings in social epistemology, whether they are compatible, and what commitments the social models force us to accept with regards to contextualisation of vice and virtue and consequentialism.

limiting information sources, evidence taken into account or blindness to alternative theories. These factors diversify the epistemic activities of the community. If there are such grounds to taking diversity and in fact epistemic vice to have beneficial effects in science, does the social interpretation conflict with these results?

First, I would like to note that in some of the models, such as Zollman's, the positive effects of dogmatism are only temporary, and their presence over the long term would hinder the possibility of convergence, which would be in agreement with the temporal aspect of good sense. So it is best to see these accounts as suggesting that epistemic vice could only locally and temporarily be advantageous to the community so long as it counteracts conservatism in the community.

Second, while these accounts suggest that in certain situations it might be advantageous for scientists to be prejudiced towards their own ideas, it is also important to emphasise that the negative effects of bias are mitigated via the social structure of science. As Helen Longino (1990) has argued, science has structures in place to identify, isolate and amend the negative effects of individual biases, ensuring that even if at the level of agents individuals hold biased and dogmatic views, at the collective level biases can be identified and eliminated via a democratic process of systematic and open criticism. The effects of individual biases can then be mitigated because the community can identify such biases and correct them. The more democratic and diverse a discipline, the more its participants can identify biases operating in their community, as has been the case with exposing sexist and racial biases in the medical sciences, for instance.[16]

Third, and most importantly, we need to acknowledge the different levels at which we can find diversity and uniformity as advantageous for scientific pursuit. We have already stressed that, according to some of the models promoting diversity, the positive effects of bias have limited application and are not seen as beneficial in the long run. But we also can appreciate that the application of the vices has different aims, in the social models the focus has been on how theories are generated, thus the emphasis on diversity. Duhem, on the other hand, is aiming to offer a way of justifying an epistemic attitude towards a theory in light of evidence, and in this sense biases seem to hinder the decision-making process. Scientists sticking to their own ideas and disregarding evidence will harm scientific progress, so open-mindedness and timidity pay off for the acceleration of progress by allowing them to reach consensus as to which

---

[16] Mann (2020) documents the effects of racial and gender bias in medical diagnoses. Criado-Perez (2019) further offers an illuminating study of gender biases in medical trials.

move to accept and how to accommodate the problematic experimental result. Going back to Kuhn (1962) is helpful here, as his distinction between normal and revolutionary science isolates what attitudes are important in each process. It pays off being a maverick during extraordinary science, but during normal science scientists are better off staying partial and conforming to the paradigm within which they work.

Last, we can also worry about the significance of virtues for reaching convergence: are they necessary and sufficient? The work of Miriam Solomon (2001) and Boaz Miller (2013) suggests that virtues are not necessary for convergence. This is because convergence can happen in the community for bad reasons, for instance a group of similarly biased individuals can converge on the same theory (historically male physicians converged on the programme that tried to find biological explanations for what was perceived as female's intellectual inferiority) and convergence can even be accidental. I think even this worry can be overcome by acknowledging that moral virtues are just some of the attributes involved in the function of good sense. Duhem emphasises that other conditions need to be in place, such as an empirically adequate theory to start with, and the virtues can be seen to make convergence more likely even if they do not necessitate it (as argued in Paternotte and Ivanova 2017).

In this section we have seen that Duhem identifies two alternative routes to resolving the holistic problem of theory testing: some scientists will look for the error in the auxiliaries while others will be more eager to question the theory being tested. He emphasises that we need further evidence to support the employment of a new hypothesis or to conclusively discard another. But he also makes an interesting move when he involves the use of intuition – good sense – a notion born out of his own scientific practice and familiarity with experimental procedures.

Judgements as to where we should be looking to isolate errors in the experiment are arrived at by stepping outside deductive logic or experimental evidence; they involve a practice cultivated form of intuition that the experimenter will employ when deciding whether to pursue a timid or a bold path. Both paths are equally valid, but it is down to the community to agree where they should put their efforts. Given the fact that different scientists can have different insights into how to proceed in addressing the negative experimental result, we need to consider their motivations: are they driven by bias, self-interest or dogmatism, or are they open-minded and humble?

We have examined the complexities behind Duhem's notorious solution to holism – the concept of good sense – and considered a number of ways to understand it. Despite the readings we have explored, the reader might still wonder if Duhem has offered a resolution here, since good sense has not given us specific tools we can use to go about locating error. Such is the aspiration of the contemporary solutions to Duhem's problem, the focus of the next section of this Element.

4 Solutions to Duhem's Problem: Diagnosing Error

Duhem's problem calls for a way in which we can determine which of the hypotheses we have used to derive a prediction is to be abandoned when the evidence we obtain contradicts the prediction. As we saw, Duhem recognises that in practice two moves can be legitimised and are used in science – sometimes modifications are made to the auxiliaries, and at other times more substantial changes are made and the testing hypothesis is modified or abandoned. A solution to Duhem's problem thus should accommodate this fact that in practice sometimes the timid move is justified and at other times it is the bold one that is needed.

Philosophers such as Popper and Imre Lakatos have traditionally offered a more one-dimensional solution because they recommend one of these moves as more suitable. Popper calls for the rejection of our testing theory in light of negative evidence while Lakatos calls for protecting the hard core, the testing theory, when our experimental outcomes do not fit those entailed by the theory. As we saw in the previous section, Duhem wants to justify both timidity and boldness as suitable responses to an anomaly. In this section we examine solutions to Duhem's problem that exhibit the flexibility Duhem called for. I start with Dorling's Bayesian solution that aims to show how the abandonment of a theory or an auxiliary hypothesis can be justified rationally by following the probability calculus. I discuss some difficulties of this account, challenging whether it can give insights into solving the problem. I then focus on two solutions that I find particularly fruitful: Darden's diagnostic solution followed by Mayo's error statistic approach. While these solutions are different, I find important commonalities in their insight into offering strategies of how to isolate error to resolve Duhem's problem. I discuss the merits of both accounts and evaluate the extent to which they align with some of Duhem's own perspectives on the solution. Last, I discuss Marcel Weber's solution to Duhem's problem that appeals to inference to the best explanation and examine its merits and limitations.

4.1 Dorling's Bayesian Solution

The Bayesian framework offers a form of inference that can tell us how learning new information should affect our confidence in a hypothesis. Let us take the following relationships between the theory T and the evidence e: $Pr(T)$ stands for the prior probability, the probability we assign the theory before knowing the evidence; $Pr(T|e)$ is the posterior probability, the probability assignment we give the theory after we have learned the new evidence; $Pr(e|T)$ is the probability of the evidence given the theory; and Pr(e) is the probability of the evidence independently of the theory. Bayes' theorem gives us the relationship between the theory and new evidence, in particular how we should change our confidence in the theory upon learning new information:

Pr(T|e) = Pr(T).Pr(e|T) | Pr(e)

Jon Dorling (1979) proposes that one of the advantages to the Bayesian framework is that it offers a solution to Duhem's problem.[17] We can formulate Duhem's problem in the following way: a conjunction of hypotheses [say Hμ and Hv] entail a prediction E; however, the experiment obtains a different result, [E*]. We are testing Hμ so we are interested in how the negative evidence affects our belief in it [Pr(Hμ|E*)], but what the holistic nature of the test entails is the condemnation of the entire conjunct in light of the obtained evidence. It has told us that Pr(E*|Hμ&Hv) = 0.

This does not give us information on which hypothesis is likely false, however. Dorling uses Bayes' theorem together with subjective probability assignments to show how E* affects the likelihoods of the individual hypotheses, Hμ and Hv. What is needed is assigning subjective probabilities to P(Hμ), Pr(Hv), Pr(E*| Hμ & ~Hv), Pr(E*|~Hμ&Hv) and Pr(E*|~Hμ&~Hv). What is assumed is that Pr(E*| Hμ&Hv) = 0, Pr(E|Hμ&Hv) = 1 and Hμ and Hv are probabilistically independent. Then Dorling can show that under certain probability assignments, one can justify discarding the auxiliary, while under other assignments it is the theory that needs to be abandoned.

The solution shows that if one starts with a considerably higher prior degree of belief in Hμ in comparison to Hv (say a probability assignment of 0.9), and Hv is regarded as more probable than not (say a probability assignment of 0.6), then by using Bayes' theorem one can compute the effect E* has on our confidence in Hμ and Hv and see that the evidence has dramatically asymmetric effects on the posterior probability of the theory and the auxiliary assumptions. By using the Bayesian framework, it is argued, we can show that the negative result affected very negligibly our confidence in the theory over the auxiliaries.

Dorling's (1979) solution presents a neat way to represent how an agent's degrees of belief change in light of new evidence and under what conditions one would be rationally justified to discard auxiliaries over theory and vice versa. If one starts with relatively low confidence in the auxiliaries by comparison to the confidence assigned to the theory being tested, Bayes' theorem shows that confidence in the theory does not diminish in light of the

---

[17] In my presentation I refrain from going into the technical details and extract the philosophical significance of the arguments. Those interested in the technical aspect of this argument should see Dorling (1979) or Mayo's (1996) accessible presentation of the formalism and proofs.

negative evidence; rather our confidence in the auxiliaries becomes significantly lower.

Dorling's solution captures our requirement to provide a flexible solution to Duhem's problem. It shows under which conditions we should be blaming the theory and under which we should be modifying auxiliaries. It is also mathematically elegant and can incorporate within its formal framework any form of information and give comparative measures of our degrees of belief. However, there are two difficulties usually directed towards this solution. First, we can question whether Dorling's solution has the resources to direct us to where we should look to allocate blame. Second, it is questioned whether this account captures how scientists actually reason, doubting the solution has descriptive merit. Let us examine these two problems in more detail.

An objection often directed at the Bayesian solution is that it offers a reconstruction of, rather than a solution to, Duhem's problem. While this framework can reconstruct certain inferences probabilistically, it does not tell us where to start looking to locate the error in the inference. One problem is that the result one obtains with regard to which hypothesis to discard is very much contingent on the prior probability assignments, but where do these prior probabilities come from? In the words of Isaac Levi, 'Bayesians need to tell us where they get their numbers from' (1982, 387). If we take the prior probability assignments to be reflective of the agent's degrees of belief, like the subjectivist Bayesians do, then these are accused of being contingent and unstable. As these are personal degrees of belief, different scientists can assign different degrees of belief to the same hypothesis, but also the very same agent can assign different probability across different times.[18]

Colin Howson and Peter Urbach respond that it is outside the Bayesian framework's aims to 'legislate' on what grounds agents arrive at their prior beliefs, and in this respect Bayesianism is seen as no different to other forms of inference. For instance, they argue, following deductive reasoning in itself also does not inform us on where the propositions in the inference come from. What the inference tells us is what conclusion follows from assumed premises. What this framework aims at, and succeeds in doing, they claim, is to offer an account of inference from the evidence, and it shows that it is irrational not to follow the probability calculus (1989, 75). As Howson and Urbach state:

---

[18] The fact that agents have unstable and often incommensurable preferences and beliefs across different times poses a number of worries for the Bayesian framework and decision theory. Paul has developed some of these problems in her illuminating book *Transformative Experience* (2014). For a helpful discussion of these implications and solutions, see Pettigrew (2020).

The Bayesian theory of support is a theory of how the acceptance as true of some evidential statement affects your belief in some hypothesis. How you came to accept the truth of the evidence, and whether you are correct in accepting it as true, are matters which, from the point of view of the theory, are simply irrelevant. (272)

Ronald Fisher (1947, 6–7) has accused the Bayesian framework of being 'useless' in scientific practice because the probability assignments ultimately measure merely psychological tendencies. Mayo (1996) is similarly sceptical that the Bayesian framework can offer us insight into where we need to look to locate the error in the conjunction of claims that gave rise to the anomaly. As such, we can see Dorling's solution more as a reconstruction of the Duhem problem, which gives little insight into how we should proceed in light of an anomalous experimental result. Mayo argues that:

[T]he Bayesian tools do not tell us what we want to know in science. What we seek are ampliative rules for generating and analysing data and for using data to learn about experimental processes in a reliable and intersubjective manner. The kinds of tools needed to do this are crucially different from those the Bayesians supply. (71)

Apart from the difficulty to provide a convincing account of priors, the Bayesian framework has been accused of being divorced from actual scientific practice. For instance, Ronald Giere argues that empirical studies analysing scientists' reasoning reveal that scientists do not reason by applying Bayesian rules, and we should not construe actual scientists as 'Bayesian information processors' (1988, 153). Mayo similarly highlights the descriptive weakness of the Bayesian accounts, arguing that scientists do not seem to operate in Bayesian ways:

Scientists do not succeed in justifying a claim that an anomaly is due to an auxiliary hypothesis by showing how their degrees of subjective belief brought them there. Were they to attempt to do so, they undoubtedly would be told to go out and muster evidence for their claim, and in so doing, it is to non-Bayesian methods that they would turn. (1996, 109)

A further problem for Dorling's solution is noted by Strevens (2001), who argues probabilistic independence between theory and auxiliaries cannot always be assumed, a limitation Dorling himself acknowledges, which limits the scope of the solution to situations where we have good grounds to assume such probabilistic independence.[19]

---

[19] Strevens has proposed an alternative solution to Duhem's problem using the Bayesian framework in which he argues that in order to avoid situations where the evidence significantly lowers the probability of the auxiliary, testing a theory should involve only auxiliaries to which we can

The Bayesian solution boils down to showing how some prior probability assignments can justify placing blame on a particular hypothesis using Bayes' theorem. But this solution stays silent with respect to the question of what justified the assignments of these probabilities or what steps a scientist should follow in establishing where to allocate blame. The solution does not address how one is to determine their prior beliefs or where one should look after a negative evidence obtains, and while the framework can be construed by its proponents as a normative one, it is questioned whether it reflects actual scientific reasoning.

4.2 Darden's Solution

Offering a very different perspective on Duhem's problem, heavily influenced by the actual practice of science and grounded in historical episodes, Darden (1990, 1991) proposes a number of strategies that can lead to the identification of fault in a testing conjunction in light of an anomalous result. According to Darden, several strategies are available to scientists to identify fault and accommodate an anomaly, and in her detailed case study from genetics, she shows how different scientists employ a plurality of strategies in light of an anomalous experimental result. Some scientists uncover implicit assumptions in the generation of the test while others identify all the explicit components involved in the obtainment of the result and assess them independently (1991, 104). The importance of her contribution is to *decompose* the theory together with all the assumptions used in the prediction, then to identify alternative routes to testing what component is responsible for the anomalous result.

Darden proposes a 'general strategy' to account for an anomalous result, which she calls 'delineate and alter' (107). The strategy involves five steps. First, we need to make sure that the anomaly is legitimate by verifying the anomalous result is indeed correct by reproducing it. After reproducing the anomaly, the scientists are forced to re-examine all the explicit assumptions that have been made in the derivation for the prediction and revaluate them. This constitutes the second step in Darden's diagnostic proposal, during which the scientists localise all the components involved in predicting the experimental outcome and delineate the potentially faulty hypothesis.

After the localisation of potentially problematic components, Darden recommends the generation of alternative hypotheses as a third step. The generation of an alternative hypothesis can be achieved by following three different strategies: (1) 'proposing the opposite', (2) 'specialization' or (3) 'universality'. The

assign the highest possible prior probabilities. For a critical discussion of this solution, see Fitelson and Waterman (2005) and Dietrich and Honenberger (2020).

idea here is that to generate alternatives, scientists will 'delineate and alter': they will try to identify potentially problematic components and then propose an alternative or the very opposite of the component in question. This means that a scientist can decide to explore the implications of taking the negation of a certain assumption, or to reconsider its scope of applicability.

Darden claims that 'specialization is a more limited change' where the new hypothesis does not have universal quantification but is localised in its application, contrary to the latter where we take the new hypothesis to be of universal applicability in its domain (105). What is noteworthy in this discussion is Darden's emphasis on the involvement of judgement: 'When a hypothesis to account for an anomaly is constructed, the decision must be made whether it is a universal, or a more limited, change to the component to be altered' (105). What is also important here is that these strategies can be entertained by different scientists and communities, but also by the very same scientist.

The fourth step in Darden's solution is to evaluate and assess the alternative hypotheses, and finally step five is to compare how the new hypothesis squares with the evidence. Here scientists decide which strategy has given the best alternative hypothesis responsible for the anomaly, or they withhold judgement. The conservative and radical strategies resonate with Duhem's own response to holism. Philosophers have had different advice on which strategy is recommended. As noted previously, for Lakatos we should always aim to alter the hypothesis that affects our established beliefs the least, unless our research programme has entered degeneration. For others, such as Popper, we are recommended to take a radical strategy and modify significantly our theoretical commitments by rejecting the established theory or paradigm in light of a new one. But Darden stresses the importance of pursuing several strategies, resonating with how Duhem describes the scientist's reaction to an anomaly. She proposes that we 'devise a set of plausible candidates' and explore these different routes at the same time (107).

To illustrate this account, Darden discusses the case of Lucien Cuénot's breeding experiments on mice, which did not agree with the predictions of Mendelian genetics. Cuénot crossed yellow hybrids (heterozygotes), knowing that the yellow colour was dominant, but the ratio he obtained in the next generation deviated from the expected 3:1; rather it was 2.55:1. After breeding this generation, he obtained no homozygous yellow mice (99). Darden identifies the strategies employed to accommodate this anomaly. Three main solutions were proposed, all of which followed the localisation strategy by trying to identify problematic components. As a matter of fact, all three accounts identified the same problematic component: they questioned the theory's account of segregation that was assumed in the prediction of the ratios. The accounts differed in how they addressed the problematic component.

Cuénot's solution to the anomaly is what Darden calls 'specialize and add'. He questioned the previously assumed hypothesis that all germ cells combine randomly and specialised it: he argued that only some germ cells combine randomly, while others show selective fertilisation.

Similarly, W. E. Caste specialised another assumption used in the derivation of the prediction: that not all combinations were equally viable. While choosing to question a different component, his strategy was a timid one where he assumed that some but not all of the combinations were viable (105). Hunt Morgan, on the other hand, who already had a critical attitude towards Mendelian genetics, employed a bolder strategy by calling into question an important assumption of the theory – the purity of the gametes. Darden argues that this was a radical move. Contrary to the strategy of specialisation, which aims to preserve as much of the commitments as possible intact, the strategy of 'proposing the universality of the opposite' aimed to revise more substantially the theoretical system in question.

Darden's framework illustrates that in practice scientists focus on different components of the theory in order to accommodate an anomaly. Cuénot questioned the random component and Morgan questioned the purity assumption, while Castle questioned the assumption about equal viability. Darden concludes: 'These alternative modifications show the usefulness of delineating the separable components and uncovering implicit ones, so that alternative modifications can be considered in the different components if an anomaly arises' (104).

In their discussion of Darden's solution, Michael Dietrich and Phillip Honenberger (2020) suggest that one limitation of this solution is the fact that it directs us to localise error in the theoretical system used for the derivation of the prediction, while we know the Duhem problem also threatens theoretical assumptions that pertain to the construction of the experiment itself. They argue that 'the search for the source of fault need not, and should not, overlook the possibility of experimental error' (343). However, while their observation is correct, I find this not to be an insurmountable worry, since Darden's approach can simply recommend for us to decompose theoretical assumptions involved in the construction of the experiment and the extraction of its results as well.

I think there is a potentially more serious worry for Darden's solution that regards the idea that at any point a scientist can decompose the testing conjunction and identify all the components involved in the generation of the prediction. Ideally, we would like this to be possible, for any individual to be able to uncover the explicit or implicit assumptions they made in the generation of a prediction. But while this may be more straightforward in some cases, it might be rather difficult in others. Here I am concerned with the nature of what an implicit assumption is and whether an individual scientist can identify such assumptions in any situation.

If such an assumption concerns, for instance, a metaphysical or philosophical idea of what an explanation should look like, perhaps a scientist upon reflection can identify and reconsider it. But sometimes an implicit assumption can be more problematic if it is, for example, an instance of implicit bias held by an individual. Biases are problematic exactly because they are implicit; individuals are unaware that they hold them.[20]

We can recall the case of craniology and the systematic efforts to locate the source for what was considered to be female intellectual inferiority. Scientists resorted to a long effort of ad hoc accommodations exactly because they were unable to identify the underlying assumption, born out of gender bias, that women are intellectually inferior to men. As we have seen in the previous section, this problem can be resolved, but only once we look into the social structure of science. What is interesting for our discussion here is whether such decomposition, as proposed by Darden, is always possible and what such decomposition would entail. While I think her proposal holds a lot of promise, it is worth noting that perhaps we need to consider the decomposition of testing hypotheses from the perspective of groups, rather than individuals, if we take the lessons from Longino's work, discussed in the previous section, on how biases are identified and eliminated in scientific practice.

Darden's account offers us a diversity of strategies we can employ when faced with an anomaly. It recognises that these strategies are often used in parallel and can be employed not just by different scientists and communities, but also by the very same scientist herself. The appeal to explore alternative solutions to the anomaly is important, contrary to the monistic solutions often entertained in the literature. The need for judgement and evaluation are also noteworthy, an aspect Duhem was eager to emphasise in the response to an experimental anomaly.

4.3 Mayo's Error Statistics Solution

Duhem shows that if we follow logic alone, in light of an anomalous result, we cannot allocate blame onto the hypothesis we are testing or any of the auxiliary assumptions. Logic does not discriminate between the individual claims or tell us which one is more likely at fault. Mayo starts with the observation that 'we know formal logic is not all we have at our disposal' (1996, 102). The problem

---

[20] For an exploration of the nature of implicit bias, see Brownstein and Saul (2016).

that remains is of an epistemic nature and concerns our reasoning for allocating error, and for this, Mayo argues, we can provide effective strategies for resolution. As previously noted, Mayo challenges the Bayesian solution to Duhem's problem for failing to offer guidance or methods by which we could start resolving the problem. Mayo aims to offer a solution that both suggests specific strategies to employ when faced with an anomaly, and reflects scientific practice by describing how scientists have gone about resolving the problem.

At the centre of Mayo's error statistics solution to Duhem's problem is the idea that we can learn from error, and in fact the aim of science should not be avoiding error, but rather identifying error and learning from it. Confidence in hypotheses is placed only if they have survived severe testing and alternative explanations have been discarded for failing such testing. To start with, let us briefly explore the different insights Mayo shares with Popper, Kuhn and the new experimentalists, but also the important ways in which their accounts part ways.

Starting with Popper's falsificationism, which takes severe testing to be constitutive of the genuine nature of science, Mayo argues that this emphasis on severe tests is well placed. However, falsificationism does not have the resources to distinguish when we should question our background assumptions rather than our theory when it fails to pass a severe test. As such, falsificationism does not tell us how to learn from error due to its insistence on changing the theories and questions we work with upon finding errors. And Lakatos, Mayo argues, who tried to amend this problem with the separation of 'hard core' and 'protective belt', does not offer an indication as to when a research programme needs to be abandoned. On Mayo's account, by severely testing a hypothesis we learn something important – when a hypothesis passes a severe test we learn also that an alternative hypothesis has failed, so 'failing as well as passing, the present account accentuates the positive' (1996, 11).

Mayo also draws our attention to the lessons we learn from Kuhn and the experimentalist turn. A crucial idea we learn from Kuhn is the significance of normal science during which science develops its experimental tools for resolving anomalies and further advancing the paradigm. Mayo questions the distinction between two different scientific activities (revolutionary and normal science), arguing that science should be seen as a process of systematic and severe testing and learning from error: 'there is just normal science, understood as standard testing' (55).

The emphasis on experimental knowledge and techniques is also motivated by the work of new experimentalism. The 1980s saw a significant shift in philosophical analysis; while previous philosophical engagement had focused predominantly on scientific theories and their ability to obtain knowledge of the world, the new experimentalists shifted the focus to the experiments and the inferences they can justify, often in the absence of theories. The influential work of Nancy Cartwright (1983), Ian Hacking (1983), Alan Franklin (1996) and Peter Galison (1987) revealed the importance of considering the philosophical questions specifically at the level of experimentation, with Hacking's famous claim that experiment has a 'life of its own' (1983, vii).[21] One main lesson we learn from this work is that experimentalists can establish the reality of entities and processes by independent means without necessarily appealing to a specific theory and that the aim of experiments can be diverse, not simply to confirm or disconfirm a theory, as previously construed (Arabatzis 2008).

Mayo takes these insights and aims to provide a framework to accommodate the lessons the new experimentalism has taught us. One of the central ideas behind her account is that we should take an experiment to support a theoretical claim only when the claim has passed severe tests – that is, when we have considered ways in which the claim can be at error and these ways have been experimentally investigated. A severe test is a test that a hypothesis is highly unlikely to pass were this hypothesis false.

An important aspect of Mayo's account is the recognition of the complexity of scientific reasoning, the idea that between the observation of raw data and the scientific hypotheses, there are important steps of scientific modelling involving the primary scientific hypothesis, experimental models and the data models (1996, 129). The idea that background assumptions are often very well warranted goes back to Giere's idea about auxiliary hypotheses embodied in instruments: 'Scientific knowledge of the technology used in experimentation is far more reliable than their knowledge of the subject matter of their experiments' (1988, 139). Mayo adds to Giere's insight that we should also consider more generally the experimental tools, such as previously encountered errors and the accumulated experimental strategies to get around these errors that give confidence in the reliability of the auxiliaries.

Mayo (1996, 1997) argues that the error statistical approach can offer us two important steps to follow when faced with Duhem's problem. The first step scientists follow when faced with a negative result from their experiment is to ensure that the experiment is sufficiently controlled and there are no intervening factors in obtaining the result so that they have ensured the anomaly is real rather than an artefact of the experimental setting. The second step after ensuring the reality of the detected effect is to distinguish warranted from

---

[21] In fact Hacking (1992) points out that Duhem's problem does not only concern the idea that a theory can always be saved from refutation by revising the auxiliary hypotheses, but also by interfering with the experimental apparatus so the experimental results are in agreement with the prediction.

unwarranted assignments of blame by establishing the significance of the testing process itself – how well does it warrant our inferences by establishing its statistical significance and margin of error? This stage ultimately establishes whether the test is a good test for the theory and the auxiliaries. As Mayo argues, 'when scientists decide to blame auxiliary over theory, they need to ensure that this claim passes severe test' (1996, 457).

According to this approach, we no longer need to see all hypotheses in a testing conjunction as equally condemned by the anomalous result, since our confidence in the particular conjunct can be very different: some hypotheses can be well grounded since they have passed severe testing, while others can be less so. Here reconsidering our confidence in the testing process, the possibility of false negatives, the margin of error and alternative hypotheses passing severe testing can all inform us when we try to localise blame.

The error statistical approach to resolving Duhem's problem is illustrated with the 1919 solar eclipse expeditions that aimed to test Einstein's prediction that the gravitational force of the sun would deflect light rays. Two expeditions were carried out to perform the observations. Sir Arthur Eddington and Sir Frank Watson Dyson led an expedition to the island of Príncipe while Andrew Crommelin and Charles Davidson led an expedition to Sobral.

Mayo argues that the analysis of the obtained results took two steps. First, agreement needed to be reached on whether the obtained results were real, and in order to discard the possibility that the deflection effect could be an artefact. This was done by using statistical procedures. Second, it needed to be established whether this effect was indeed due to gravitational effects, as predicted by Einstein's theory, or whether a different factor accounted for the observed effect, which would be in agreement with the Newtonian theory of gravity (238).

The first step of the reasoning was to establish whether the effect was real, and on this Newtonian and Einsteinian proponents agreed that the plate readings reported a genuine phenomenon. However, initially, there was space for doubt. The photographic plates obtained from the Sobral observations of the eclipse presented an anomaly that brought Einstein's predictions into question, but Eddington's strategy was first to question whether there was an error in the way the evidence was obtained, 'whether there were grounds for error – either in the data or in the background factors assumed not to be responsible' (458).

Mayo once again stresses that prior beliefs were irrelevant when the scientists turned their attention to this anomaly – that is, it was irrelevant whether scientists' loyalties sat with Einstein or Newton. What played a role in resolving the significance of the anomaly was having the appropriate tools with which to distinguish whether the anomaly was simply noise or an artefact of the reading.

By analysing the data, the scientists were able to detect that the results were distorted by the mirror used in the photographs. Mayo argues that error statistics offered the tools for analysing the results and isolating the error; this knowledge is a result of other astronomical experiments that have been previously successfully carried out.

This focus on the experimental knowledge obtained and the analysis of results is what carries on in scientific practice and gives justification for certain inferences. This strategy is possible because we have enough experimental knowledge from previous experiments to discern error coming from mirror distortion from a deflection effect. As Mayo argues: 'Duhem's problem is built on the supposition that an error or anomaly is silent about its source – and indeed it is silent when approached by the white glove of logical analysis. But in the hands of shrewd inquisitors of error it may be made to speak volumes, and often a whisper is enough to distinguish its source from others' (458–9).

The next step in the reasoning is to establish why the plate readings speak in favour of Einstein's theory. Here scientists consider if there are other explanations of the observed effect. Indeed, a number of 'Newtonian saving factors' were proposed to account for the observations, including an assumption that the light deflection was due to the cooling effect of the moon's shadow. To establish the plausibility of these Newtonian saving factors, the community had to establish whether these alternative explanations withstood severe testing. In particular, it needed to be established whether the proposed saving factors were significant enough to account for the observed effect, and if the effect was taken to be significant enough to account for the observed deflection, whether any problematic implications followed.

By following these two steps, the scientists were able to discard the proposed adjusting hypotheses on the grounds that they failed severe testing. In the case of the cooling effect of the moon, in particular, the implied temperature drop was much more significant from the observed, making it highly implausible. Mayo argues that in each case, the arguments were seriously considered and their implications tested using a body of knowledge from error probabilities of procedures.

Once again Mayo contrasts her solution with the Bayesian one, arguing that were we to follow the Bayesian approach in this case, when accounting for the observed deflection, proponents of Newton could have interpreted the result to only slightly decrease their confidence in the theory. But their prior confidence in the theory is irrelevant, Mayo contends, for the evaluation of the success of their strategies – which were to blame external factors over Newton's theory. But the evaluation of these other factors was established by how well they stood severe testing, and they were discarded when they failed to do so. Mayo argues that 'the concern was with a classic error – that the evidence failed to construct a reliable test in favor of the auxiliary factor hypothesized to accommodate the anomaly' (457).

While Mayo argues that not every episode of the Duhemian problem will allow for such a resolution – for instance, it might be difficult to meet the second strategy – the insights offered in her analysis are a way to recognise how scientists, at least sometimes, resolve such situations successfully and to acknowledge that the resolution relies on tools that come from error statistics rather than from thinking about the inference from priors to posteriors via Bayes' theorem.

Mayo's account recognises the layers of theorising and modelling involved in extracting meaningful evidence from the data, the piecemeal nature of scientific tests and the importance of offering specific tools for discriminating when faced with an anomaly as to where to allocate blame. Her account shares the virtues of being informed by detailed studies of instructive historical episodes where scientists confronted an anomaly and found themselves faced with Duhem's problem, and she successfully illustrates the shortcoming of seeing these historical episodes through the lenses of the Bayesian account.

Mayo has offered several steps that have been and can be used successfully in delineating when an anomaly should be taken to be legitimate rather than noise, and under what conditions we can see such an anomaly to speak against the theory we are testing rather than in the auxiliaries involved in the test. These judgements are a product of our knowledge of experimental practices and procedures, knowledge that accumulates and acts as the backbone in our learning from experimental results.

4.4 Holism and Inference to the Best Explanation

Marcel Weber proposes a resolution to Duhem's problem using inference to the best explanation (IBE), the main idea being that while it is possible for one or more auxiliary hypotheses to be wrong in the derivation of an experimental result, if together with the theory these generate the best explanation of the experimental result by comparison to alternatives, we have good grounds to prefer them. This account allows us to say that an experiment is crucial in supporting a hypothesis if it offers the best explanation for the results.

While the Duhem problem makes us question the possibilities of such experiments, Weber believes that, at least in some cases, using IBE we can say the experiment offered the best support for a hypothesis. Let me illustrate the argument with one of the most celebrated experiments from molecular biology: the Meselson-Stahl experiment, coined by John Cairns as 'the most beautiful experiment in biology'.[22]

After the 1953 discovery of the structure of DNA molecules, the question that needed addressing was how DNA replicates. Three different mechanisms were proposed: (1) conservative replication, proposed by Gunther Stent, according to which each of the two strands of the parent DNA molecule are replicated in the new; (2) semi-conservative replication, proposed by John Watson and Francis Crick, according to which one strand of the parent DNA is conserved in the daughter DNA; and (3) dispersive replication, proposed by Max Delbrück, suggesting that the parent DNA chains break at intervals, with the parental segments combining with new segments to form the daughter DNA.

In 1958 Matthew Meselson and Franklin Stahl published the results of an experiment they had performed a year earlier that is broadly regarded to have conclusively supported the semi-conservative replication and discredited the alternative proposals. Meselson and Stahl fed bacteria nutrients containing heavy nitrogen isotope that through metabolising is incorporated into the bacterial genetic material. They continued the process until the genetic material of the bacteria became heavy. Then they fed the bacteria light nitrogen and studied the genetic material of the bacteria through the next generations.

Using ultracentrifugation to separate light from heavy genetic material, they obtained ratios of light, heavy and hybrid DNA compatible with the semi-conservative replication. They obtained a band of intermediate density in the first generation, while a combination of intermediate density and light density followed in the next generation. The results were seen to disconfirm the conservative and dispersive models of replication since the former predicts only light and heavy DNA in the next generations while the latter entails only intermediate-density DNA (Holmes 2008).

So why is this experiment considered crucial in the confirmation of the semi-conservative replication? Couldn't a proponent of the conservative strategy, for instance, insist that there was an error in the auxiliaries and the experiment cannot be regarded to disprove the conservative replication? As Weber notes, Meselson and Stahl did indeed rely on auxiliaries we now know are false, concerning an assumption that the centrifuge process does not alter the genetic material in extraction (Weber 2009, 29), although he believes these assumptions did not in fact affect the results.

Despite this Duhemian worry, Weber thinks we have good reasons to take the Meselson and Stahl experiment to support Crick and Watson's semi-

---

[22] The question of what makes this experiment aesthetically valuable is explored in Ivanova (2021).

conservative replication, but this is only possible if we step outside the constraints of deductive reasoning and employ abduction. On Weber's account, the semi-conservative replication offers the best explanation for the obtained results, by comparison to the other replication hypotheses, where best is seen as needing the minimum number of hypotheses to explain the results. Weber sees the IBE solution to explain the acceptance of this experiment among the scientific community and why it is often regarded as an example of a crucial experiment in science, claiming that 'only such [an] IBE-type of argument can make sense of the widely shared intuition ... that the Meselson-Stahl data provided strong discriminatory evidence for the semi-conservative hypothesis' (40).

What is the relationship between Weber's solution to Duhem's problem and the accounts we have discussed so far? First, when it comes to Bayesian theories of confirmation, Weber sees his account as complimentary. Samir Okasha (2000) and Peter Lipton (2004, ch. 7) already note that IBE and Bayesian personal degrees of belief are not in conflict, but Weber further suggests that we can see IBE as strengthening the Bayesian account, for instance, by offering further constraints on how prior probabilities are determined. When it comes to Mayo's error statistics, however, Weber argues for the superiority of his solution.

One difficulty for the error statistical solution, Weber contends, is that in cases like the Meselson-Stahl experiment, error statistics fail to explain why the experimental results are taken to offer good evidence for the semi-conservative replication, despite the fact that Meselson and Stahl were unable to eliminate some significant errors from the experiment. There was an important auxiliary assumption in the Meselson-Stahl interpretation of the data that was only later evidentially supported. This fact would lead proponents of the error statistics approach not to admit that the original experiment offered evidence in support of semi-conservative replication, which goes against, Weber argues, how scientists themselves see the significance of the results.

In particular, Meselson and Stahl were unable to eliminate a major error from their experiment in 1958. Weber argues that the experiment technically shows the symmetrical distribution of heavy nitrogen during the replication, but not that the bands, from which density distributions were inferred, correspond to single DNA duplexes. 'It was technically possible that the intermediate band represents an end-to-end association of parental DNA duplexes with newly synthesised duplexes rather than a hybrid molecule composed of a light and a heavy strand (this would make the results compatible with the conservative hypothesis)' (2009, 32). The alternative interpretation that Meselson and Stahl had ruled out was experimentally supported later.

Weber acknowledges that a proponent of the error statistical solution could simply respond by claiming that Meselson and Stahl did not have good evidence of the semi-conservative replication until they had subjected the alternative reading to severe testing, obtained later by Ron Rolfe's experiments, but for Weber this would not explain how the episode unfolded. Furthermore, Weber argues that we cannot in principle ever eliminate every possible error, which would not enable us to draw inferences from our experiments.

Tudor Baetu (2019) has, however, disagreed with Weber's take on this episode, arguing more in the direction of Mayo's account. For Baetu the Meselson-Stahl results were 'fragile' and the replication question did not settle in 1958. More experimental work was needed to solidify the results in favour of the semi-conservative replication and discount the conservative one. As noted earlier, the experiment relied on auxiliary assumptions that needed to be independently tested and were tested over a period beyond the original experiment.

Specifically, to interpret the obtained results, Meselson and Stahl assumed that the bands observed after centrifugation did not consist of end-to-end or laterally associated linear DNA fragments, which would be compatible with the conservative replication position. For this reason, Baetu contends that we cannot claim that the 1958 experiment conclusively discredited the alternative replication models or the idea that this very experiment conclusively favours the Crick-Watson replication model. Only after Rolfe's tests showing that DNA fragments do not reassociate in an end-to-end configuration was the assumption solidified in favour of the semi-conservative replication and against the conservative one.

Baetu thinks that the lesson we should draw here is that it is possible to overcome the holistic challenge by subjecting auxiliaries to independent tests, echoing Mayo's approach. Baetu further questions the historical reconstruction of this experiment as an example of a 'crucial experiment' in science, arguing that we should see the experiment as part of a research project with broader aims that would have been accomplished even if the competing replication models were not dismissed – that settling conclusively the question of the replication model was not the primary aim of the project:

> The historical significance of the Meselson-Stahl experiment had little to do with the expectations raised by the crucial experiment account. The primary goal of the experiment was to provide information about the transfer of atoms from parent to daughter DNA, information in turn required to gain further insights into the chemical reactions involved in DNA synthesis. This object-ive could have been achieved irrespective of the rejection of rival hypotheses, and some information would have been gained even if none of the candidate hypotheses would have been conclusively supported. (410)

While Weber sees the Meselson-Stahl experiment as challenging Mayo's solution, Baetu's analysis helps us to see how this case can be understood via the error statistic approach. The original experiment relied on an assumption that needed further testing, a fact Meselson and Stahl recognised themselves, thus inviting their student Rolfe to continue with the experimental tests. Thus, to conclusively dismiss conservative replication, the Meselson-Stahl experiment could only do so after further testing was done, making the original experiment inconclusive, rather than a crucial experiment, as it is usually read.

A further objection to Weber's solution to holism concerns the very use of IBE. This form of inference has been challenged by van Fraassen's (1989) 'bad lot' objection, undermining the idea that selecting the best explanation from a pool of considered candidates correlates with their truthlikeless, since the explanation can still turn out to be the best one from a pool of bad contenders.

This solution faces the problem that ultimately what constitutes 'the best explanation' is expected to vary and it might not always be possible to rank all best explanations among a pool of actual and possible contenders. While Weber believes that by adopting a mechanistic account of explanation we can place a significant constraint on which explanations are considered legitimate, the solution becomes limited and is not obviously required in many situations where we face the Duhem problem. Furthermore, I worry to what extent Weber needs to introduce IBE in his reasoning, rather than merely simplicity considerations. What we see in the Meselson-Stahl example is that the 1958 experimental results could be accounted for by two competing hypotheses: conservative replication and semi-conservative replication with an additional assumption. What seems to be happening in our selection of the former hypothesis over the latter is merely arguing that simplicity considerations are at play when we decide how to interpret the result, and it remains unclear how this selection is a form of inference to the best explanation.

5 Conclusion

This Element started with an analysis of Duhem's outlook on scientific methodology and the aims of science. We saw that the starting point for Duhem's problem is the reflection on scientific methodology and the claim that science follows the deductive method with its explicitly defined steps. But by following this method we are led to the problem of holism, the idea that our experiments cannot conclusively condemn or support the hypotheses we test, thus undermining our confidence that we can learn from experience. Duhem's problem, while arising from an attempt to see scientific reasoning and inferences following specific steps and being subject to rules, gives rise to the worry that scientific reasoning might not be formalisable after all, that certain situations in practice deviate significantly from our ideal to break down and specify the steps we need to follow to reach a decision. Duhem resorts to arguing that part of scientific reasoning cannot be captured by rules; on the contrary, judgement and intuition are invoked to resolve the problem and to isolate which hypothesis is to blame for the anomalous experimental result.

We have explored Duhem's concept of good sense that he offers in response to his holistic thesis. In the absence of rules Duhem resorts to seeing a solution to the problem in the scientists themselves, their traits and their ability to act as impartial and diligent judges in choosing which hypothesis to select as problematic. This shift in his analysis, from thinking about the process of inquiry to thinking about the individual, has generated a number of different interpretations that see Duhem's concept as a virtue-theoretic one. But while we can appreciate that these reconstructions have helped us gain more systematic insight into how Duhem might have understood this notion, it is contentious whether this notion can indeed be seen as a solution, as anything beyond a story we retrospectively tell about specific historical instances where scientists navigated through such a problem.

I have defended a reconstruction of this concept in my attempt to understand what it would need to look like to achieve the goal Duhem set out to achieve. However, it remains challenging to see the concept of good sense as a solution, as a concept that can guide scientists in resolving the holistic problem. One of the issues here pertains to the problem that it is not clear exactly what we expect to find in a solution to Duhem's problem. Is a concept, such as scientists' good sense, or any other idealised concept such as a perfect moral agent or an ideal scientist, informative and normatively strong enough to do the work we need it to do? What would constitute a satisfactory solution to Duhem's problem?

Addressing this problem is crucial when we evaluate whether we consider the contemporary solutions to Duhem's problem to indeed offer a resolution. We have seen that despite Bayesians' enthusiasm, the framework does little to address the problem at hand, and in an important sense seems vacuous. For while it can seem to reconstruct the problem, we have little reason to think this account describes how we actually act as agents faced with an experimental anomaly, and the approach seems to do little in terms of giving guidance as to how we should proceed when faced with this problem.

Darden's and Mayo's accounts certainly go some way in offering us insights into how scientists often resolve such situations and extract lessons from specific historical examples. Darden proposes an analytical strategy that advises us to decompose a system to all of its components so they can be independently evaluated. We are advised to pursue this evaluation by considering a different scope to a potentially problematic hypothesis, by restricting its applicability, generalising it or suggesting the opposite, in order to evaluate its fit with the data.

Mayo, on the other hand, asks us to consider the breadth of experimental knowledge and procedures in order to evaluate which hypotheses are better supported by the experimental tests they have undergone, given that error statistical methods can tell us how good a test is to detect certain errors. We are advised to only trust hypotheses that have undergone severe testing. Our trust in an hypothesis has little to do with prior assignments of probabilities; rather, it is our experimental knowledge and statistical procedures that tell us what hypotheses to trust in light of them passing severe testing, testing the hypothesis cannot pass were it false. So while Duhem's problem in its logical formulation puts equal blame on all the hypotheses in the tested conjunction, Mayo insightfully argues that we have at our disposal more than logic to decide between hypotheses depending on the testing they have passed. When faced with an anomaly, then, it makes good sense to start by evaluating hypotheses that have not withstood severe testing.

Last, Weber's account also emerges from a detailed case study and shows how utilising simplicity considerations can help us decide between competing readings of an experimental result. While I have expressed some worries as to whether the account does more than simply tell us such considerations are important to ground our decision in how we read the experiment, it is clear that even here we have a sense of flexibility with respect to how scientists utilise and settle among such considerations, leaving space for judgement.

The last three proposals outlined here, while different in nature, share important insights. They stay close to scientific practice and refrain from advocating a universal solution. Rather, they offer guiding principles that can be employed when we are faced with an anomaly and justify why we would question some hypotheses over others first. The important issue to focus on next is to evaluate how successful these solutions are, and whether they have overcome the shortcomings of Duhem's own solution.

I have already argued that if we are looking for a generalised normative solution, we have not found it in any of the accounts, and it is dubious whether such a solution is possible. But these accounts have offered us, together, a plurality of strategies that can be utilised effectively in practice. I have found both Darden and Mayo to have offered us insights into how we can at least sometimes go about resolving the epistemological problem Duhem's holism gives rise to and locate which hypotheses to examine first.

In this sense, while the logical formulation to Duhem's holism seems unresolvable since it condemns equally all the hypotheses in the testing conjunct, the epistemological question of whether we have good grounds to trust certain hypotheses over others seems to be productively addressed by Darden's and Mayo's strategies. It is important to note that both solutions assume that auxiliary hypotheses can be subjected to testing in isolation, which can be seen to be exactly what the holistic thesis denies. But what these solutions highlight is that the assumptions we make in the derivation of a prediction and the set-up of an experiment can have different epistemic weight and can be subjected to independent tests, and much of our confidence in an assumption can come from a body of well-established experimental procedures.

And yet, when we compare these solutions to Duhem's contentious notion of good sense, we find that some of Duhem's sentiments have carried over. As we have already noted, the notion of good sense does capture some important insights: the idea that bias and self-interest can be an obstacle to scientists arriving at a solution; the question of how scientists reach consensus when they face anomalous results; and the recognition of the role of judgement and intuition in science, and whether some actions in science can in principle be adequately captured by rules.

Darden's solution certainly does not seem to have gotten rid of the involvement of judgement in the resolution of holism, for while decomposing a theoretical framework into its constituents and investigating each part seems well advised, the process of evaluation and assessment (the fourth and fifth steps in her strategy) leaves space for individual judgement. We could also make a similar observation about Mayo's solution, because even though error statistics can offer a justification for trust in some hypotheses over others, there is space for judgement in which hypotheses get tested and when we think we have eliminated all possible errors.

The Duhem problem has significant implications for science and our confidence in scientific knowledge. Experiments play a vital role in the obtainment of empirical knowledge about the world; they are meant to give us direct access to areas we cannot perceive with the senses and allow us to intervene in nature. The holistic thesis of theory testing undermines our confidence in acquiring knowledge about the world through experiment. But while Duhem formulates this problem in a logical form, he seeks a very different form of solution to the problem, leaving the logical formulation behind and identifying what scientists do when they find themselves in such situations.

Duhem's proposal reflects his own background. As a physicist concerned with methodological questions about science, he is concerned with the problem of how we extract knowledge from experiments, and when we decide an experiment has decisively spoken in favour of or against a hypothesis. While his notion of good sense is often found to be a troubling aspect of his general philosophy, this notion reflects something important about practice that Duhem stresses again and again. Some situations in science do not boil down to rule-following; they are open and involve individual judgement and the pursuit of alternative avenues. This Element has explored a number of contemporary accounts that address how we can respond to an anomalous experimental result. And while these accounts offered a number of specific strategies to localise blame in a testing conjunction, we saw that each of these accounts leaves some space for the exercise of judgement, preserving some of Duhem's good sense.

Bibliography

Achinstein, P. (2007). Atom's empirical Eve: Methodological disputes and how to evaluate them, *Perspectives on Science*, 15 (3), 359–90.

Achinstein, P. (1991). *Particles and Waves: Historical Essays in the Philosophy of Science*, Oxford University Press.

Arabatzis, T. (2008). Experiment. In M. Curd and S. Psillos (eds.), *The Routledge Companion to Philosophy of Science*, Routledge, 159–70.

Ariew, R. (1984). The Duhem thesis, *British Journal for the Philosophy of Science*, 35, 313–25.

Baetu, T. (2019). On the possibility of crucial experiments in biology, *British Journal for the Philosophy of Science*, 70, 407–29.

Barnes, E. C. (2008). *The Paradox of Predictivism*, Cambridge University Press.

Beauchemin, P. H. (2017). Autopsy of measurements with the ATLAS detector at the LHC. *Synthese*, 194, 275–312.

Ben-Menahem, Y. (2006). *Conventionalism: From Poincaré to Quine.* Cambridge University Press.

Bhakthavatsalam, S. (2017). Duhemian good sense and agent reliabilism, *Studies in History and Philosophy of Science*, 64, 22–9.

Bhakthavatsalam, S. (2015). The rationale behind Pierre Duhem's natural classification, *Studies in the History and Philosophy of Science*, 51, 11–21.

Boyd, R. (1983). On the current status of the issue of scientific realism, *Erkenntnis*, 19, 45–90.

Breitenbach, A. (2013). Aesthetics in science: A Kantian proposal, *Proceedings of the Aristotelian Society*, 113, 83–100.

Brenner, A. (1990). Holism a century ago: The elaboration of Duhem's thesis, *Synthese*, 83, 325–35.

Brownstein, M., and Saul, J. (2016) *Implicit Bias and Philosophy: Metaphysics and Epistemology*, Oxford University Press.

Chalmers, A. (2013). *What Is This Thing Called Science?* 3rd edition, University of Queensland Press.

Chang, H. (forthcoming). *Realism for Realistic People*, Cambridge University Press.

Coko, K. (2020). Jean Perrin and the philosophers' stories: The role of multiple determination in determining Avogadro's number, *HOPOS: The Journal of the International Society for the History of Philosophy of Science*, 10 (1), 143–93.

Coko, K. (2015). Epistemology of a believing historian: Making sense of Duhem's anti-atomism. *Studies in History and Philosophy of Science*, 50, 71–82.

Criado-Perez, C. (2019). *Invisible Women: Exposing Data Bias in a World Designed for Men*, Vintage.

Cushing, J. (1994). *Quantum Mechanics: Historical Contingency and the Copenhagen Hegemony*, University of Chicago Press.

Darden, L. (1991). *Theory Change in Science: Strategies from Mendelian Genetics*. Oxford University Press.

Darden, L. (1990). Diagnosing and fixing faults in theories. In J. Shrager and P. Langley (eds.), *Computational Models of Scientific Discovery and Theory Formation*, Morgan Kaufmann, 319–46.

Darling, K. M. (2003). Motivational realism: The natural classification for Pierre Duhem, *Philosophy of Science*, 70 (5), 1125–36.

Dietrich, M., and Honenberger, P. (2020) Duhem's problem revisited: Logical vs epistemic formulations and solutions, *Synthese*, 197, 337–54.

Dion, S. M. (2013) Pierre Duhem and the inconsistency between instrumentalism and natural classification, *Studies in History and Philosophy of Science*, 44, 12–19.

Dorling, J. (1979). Bayesian personalism, the methodology of scientific research programmes, and Duhem's problem, *Studies in History and Philosophy of Science*, 10 (3), 177–87.

Duhem, P. (1991 [1915]). *German Science: Some Reflections on German Science: German Science and German Virtues* (J. Lyon, trans.), Open Court.

Duhem, P. (1969 [1908]). *To Save the Phenomena: An Essay on the Idea of Physical Theory from Plato to Galileo* (E. Doland and C. Mascher, trans.), University of Chicago Press.

Duhem, P. (1954 [1906]). *The Aim and Structure of Physical Theory*, Princeton University Press.

Fairweather, A. (2012). The epistemic value of good sense, *Studies in History and Philosophy of Science*, 43, 139–46.

Fisher, R. A. (1947). *The Design of Experiment*, Oliver and Boyd.

Fitelson, B., and Waterman, A. (2005). Bayesian confirmation and auxiliary hypotheses revisited: A reply to Strevens. *British Journal for the Philosophy of Science*, 56, 293–302.

Franklin, A. (1986). *The Neglect of Experiment*, Cambridge University Press.

Fricker, M. (2007). *Epistemic Injustice: Power and the Ethics of Knowing*, Oxford University Press.

Galison, P. (1987). *How Experiments End*, Chicago University Press.

Giere, R. (1988). *Explaining Science*, Chicago University Press.

Gower, B. S. (2000). Cassirer, Schlick and 'structural' realism: The philosophy of the exact sciences in the background to early logical empiricism', *British Journal for the History of Philosophy*, 8, 71–106.

Grünbaum, A. (1962). The falsifiability of theories: Total or partial? A contemporary evaluation of the Duhem-Quine thesis, *Synthese*, 14, 17–34.

Hacking, I. (1992). The self-vindication of the laboratory sciences. In A. Pickering (ed.), *Science As Practice and Culture*, University of Chicago Press, 29–64.

Hacking, I. (1983). *Representing and Intervening: Introductory Topics in the Philosophy of Natural Science*, Cambridge University Press.

Hanson, N. R. (1958). *Patterns of Discovery: An Inquiry into the Conceptual Foundations of Science*, Cambridge University Press.

Harding, S. G. (ed.) (1975). *Can Theories Be Refuted? Essays on the Duhem-Quine Thesis*, Reidel.

Hoefer, C., and Rosenberg, A. (1994). Empirical equivalence, underdetermination, and systems of the World. *Philosophy of Science*, 61, 592–607.

Holmes, F. L. (2008). *Meselson, Stahl, and the Replication of DNA*, Yale University Press.

Howson, C., and Urbach, P. (1989). *Scientific Reasoning: The Bayesian Approach*, Open Court.

Hudson, R. (2020) What was Perrin really doing in his proof of the reality of atoms? *HOPOS: The Journal of the International Society for the History of Philosophy of Science*, 10, 194–218.

Hull, D. (1988). *Science As a Process: An Evolutionary Account of the Social and Conceptual Development of Science*. University of Chicago Press.

Ivanova, M. (forthcoming). Theory virtues and theory acceptance, *Lauener Series in Philosophy: Bas van Fraassen's Contribution to Philosophy of Science*.

Ivanova, M. (2021). The aesthetics of scientific experiments. *Philosophy Compass*. DOI: 10.1111/phc3.12730

Ivanova, M. (2020b). Reflections on the reception of Jean Perrin's experiments by his contemporaries, *HOPOS: The Journal of the International Society for the History of Philosophy of Science*, 219-224.

Ivanova, M. (2020a). Beauty, truth and understanding. In Milena Ivanova and Steven French (eds.) *The Aesthetics of Science: Beauty, Imagination and Understanding*, Routledge, 86–104.

Ivanova, M. (2017b). Poincaré's aesthetics of science, *Synthese*, 194, 2581–94.

Ivanova, M. (2017a). Aesthetic values in science, *Philosophy Compass*, 12. DOI: 10.1111/phc3.12433

Ivanova, M. (2015). Conventionalism about what? Where Duhem and Poincaré part ways, *Studies in the History and Philosophy of Science*, 54, 80–9.

Ivanova, M. (2014). Is there a place for epistemic virtues in theory choice? In A. Fairweather (ed.), *Virtue Scientia: Bridges between Virtue Epistemology and Philosophy of Science*, Synthese Library, 366, 207–26.

Ivanova, M. (2013). Did Perrin's experiments convert Poincaré to scientific realism? *HOPOS: The Journal of the International Society for the History of Philosophy of Science*, 3, 1–19.

Ivanova, M. (2011). 'Good sense' in context: A response to Kidd, *Studies in History and Philosophy of Science*, 42, 610–12.

Ivanova, M. (2010). Pierre Duhem's good sense as a guide to theory choice. *Studies in History and Philosophy of Science*, 41, 58–64.

Ivanova, M., and French, S. (2020). *The Aesthetics of Science: Beauty, Imagination and Understanding*, Routledge.

Ivanova, M., and Paternotte, C. (2013). Theory choice, good sense and social consensus. *Erkenntnis*, 78, 1109–32.

Kidd, I. (2011). Pierre Duhem's epistemic aims and the intellectual virtue of humility: A reply to Ivanova. *Studies in the History and Philosophy of Science*, 42, 185–9.

Kidd, I., Battaly, H. and Cassam, Q. (2020). *Vice Epistemology: Theory and Practice*, Routledge.

Kitcher, P. (1993). *The Advancement of Science: Science without Legend, Objectivity without Illusions*. Oxford University Press.

Kitcher, P. (1990). The division of cognitive labor. *Philosophy of Science*, 87, 5–22.

Kollerstrom, N. (2006) An hiatus in history: The British claim for Neptune's co-prediction, 1845–1846. Part I, *History of Science*, 44, 141–62.

Kuhn, T. (1977). Objectivity, value judgment, and theory choice. In *The Essential Tension*, University of Chicago Press, 320–53.

Kuhn, T. (1962). *The Structure of Scientific Revolutions*, University of Chicago Press.

Laudan, L., & Leplin, J. (1991). Empirical equivalence and underdetermination. *Journal of Philosophy*, 88, 269–85.

Levi, I. (1982) Ignorance, probability and rational choice, *Synthese*, 53, 387–417.

Lipton, P. (2004). *Inference to the Best Explanation*, 2nd edition, Routledge.

Longino, H. (1990). *Science As Social Knowledge: Value and Objectivity in Scientific Inquiry*. Princeton University Press.

Lugg, A. (1990). Pierre Duhem's conception of natural classification. *Synthese*, 83, 409–20.

Mann, K. (2020) *Entitled: How Male Privilege Hurts Women*, Allen Lane.

Martin, E. (1991). The egg and the sperm: How science has constructed a romance based on stereotypical male female roles. *Signs*, 16, 485–501.

Martin, R. N. D. (1991). *Pierre Duhem: Philosophy and History in the Work of a Believing Physicist*, Open Court.

Massey, G. J. (2011). Quine and Duhem on holistic hypotheses testing, *American Philosophical Quarterly*, 48, 239–66.

Mättig, P., and Stöltzner, M. (2019). Model choice and crucial tests. On the empirical epistemology of the Higgs discovery, *Studies in History and Philosophy of Modern Physics*, 65, 73–96.

Maxwell, G. (1962). The ontological status of theoretical entities. In H. Feigl and G. Maxwell (eds.), *Minnesota Studies in the Philosophy of Science*, Vol. 3, University of Minnesota Press, 3–14.

Mayo, D. G. (1997). Duhem's problem, the Bayesian way, and error statistics, or 'What's belief got to do with it?' *Philosophy of Science*, 64, 222–44.

Mayo, D. G. (1996). *Error and the Growth of Experimental Knowledge*. University of Chicago Press.

McAllister, J. (1996). *Beauty and Revolution in Science*. Cornell University Press.

McMullin, E. (2009). The virtue of a perfect theory. In M. Curd and S. Psillos (eds.), *The Routledge Companion to Philosophy of Science*, Routledge.

McMullin, E. (1990). Comment: Duhem's middle way. *Synthese*, 83, 421–30.

Meselson, M., and Stahl, F. W. (1958). The replication of DNA in Escherichia coli, *Proceedings of the National Academy of Science of the United States of America*, 44, 671–82.

Miller, B. (2013). When is consensus knowledge based? Distinguishing shared knowledge from mere agreement. *Synthese*, 190, 1293–1316.

Mongin, P. (2009). Duhemian themes in expected utility theory. In A. Brenner and J. Gayon (eds.), *French Studies in the Philosophy of Science*, Springer.

Okasha, S. (2000) Van Fraassen's critique of inference to the best explanation, *Studies in History and Philosophy of Science*, 31, 691–710.

Paternotte, C. and Ivanova, M. (2017). Virtues and vices in scientific practice. *Synthese* 194, 1787–1807.

Paul, L. (2014). *Transformative Experience*, Oxford University Press.

Pettigrew, R. (2020). *Choosing for Changing Selves*, Oxford University Press.

Pohlhaus, G., and Kidd, I. (2017). *The Routledge Handbook to Epistemic Injustice*, Routledge.

Poincaré, H. (2001 [1902]) Science and hypothesis. In S. Gould (ed.), *The Value of Science: Essential Writings of Henri Poincaré*, The Modern Library.

Poincaré, H. (1963 [1913]). *Science and Mathematics: Last Essays*. Dover.

Popper, K. (1963) *Conjectures and Refutations: The Growth of Scientific Knowledge*, Routledge.

Psillos, S. (2014). The view from within and the view from above: Looking at van Fraassen's Perrin, Bas van Fraassen's Approach to Representation and Models in Science, *Synthese Library* 36: 143–66.

Psillos, S. (1999) *Scientific Realism: How Science Tracks Truth*. Routledge.

Putnam, H. (1975). *Philosophical Papers, Vol. 1: Mathematics, Matter and Method*, Cambridge University Press.

Redhead, M. (1995). *From Physics to Metaphysics*, Cambridge University Press.

Rowbottom, D. P. (2010). Corroboration and auxiliary hypotheses: Duhem's thesis revisited, *Synthese*, 177, 139–49.

Russell, B. (1927). *The Analysis of Matter*, George Allen & Unwin.

Schindler, S. (2018). *Theory Virtues in Science: Uncovering Reality through Theory*, Cambridge University Press.

Sklar, L. (1974). *Space, Time, and Spacetime*, University of California Press.

Sober, E. (2004). Likelihood, model selection, and the Duhem-Quine problem. *The Journal of Philosophy*, 101, 221–41.

Solomon, M. (2001). *Social Empiricism*. MIT Press.

Stanford, P. K. (2006) *Exceeding Our Grasp: Science, History, and the Problem of Unconceived Alternatives*, Oxford University Press.

Strevens, M. (2003) The role of the priority rule in science. *Journal of Philosophy* 100, 55–79.

Strevens, M. (2001). The Bayesian treatment of auxiliary hypotheses. *British Journal for the Philosophy of Science*, 52, 515–37.

Stump D. (2011). The scientist as impartial judge: Moral values in Duhem's philosophy of science. New perspectives on Pierre Duhem's *The aim and structure of physical theory* (book symposium), *Metascience*, 20, 1–25.

Stump, D. (2007). Pierre Duhem's virtue epistemology. *Studies in History and Philosophy of Science*, 38, 149–59.

Todd, C. S. (2008). Unmasking the truth beneath the beauty: Why the supposed aesthetic judgments made in science may not be aesthetic at all. *International Studies in the Philosophy of Science*, 22: 61–79.

van Fraassen, B. (2009). The perils of Perrin, in the hands of philosophers. *Philosophical Studies*, 143, 5–24.

van Fraassen, B. (1989) *Laws and symmetry*. Oxford University Press.

van Fraassen, B. (1980). *The Scientific Image*, Oxford University Press.

Weber, M. (2009). The crux of crucial experiments: Duhem's problems and inference to the best explanation. *British Journal for the Philosophy of Science*, 60, 19–49.

Weisberg, M., and Muldoon, R. (2009). Epistemic landscapes and the division of labour. *Philosophy of Science*, 76, 225–52.

Worrall, J. (2009) Underdetermination, realism and empirical equivalence, *Synthese*, 180, 157–72.

Worrall, J. (1996 [1989]). Structural realism: The best of both worlds? In D. Papineau (ed.), *The Philosophy of Science*, Oxford: Oxford University Press, 139–66.

Zagzebski, L. (2003). The search for the source of epistemic good. In M. Brady and D. Pritchard (eds.), *Moral and Epistemic Virtues*, Blackwell, 13–27.

Zollman, K. J. S. (2010). The epistemic benefit of transient diversity. *Erkenntnis*, 72, 17–35.

Acknowledgements

I have been very privileged to find myself in the most stimulating and support-ive environment, and I would like to thank all the students I have worked with in the Department for History and Philosophy of Science at the University of Cambridge. It was with them in mind that this book was written in hope they will find it constructive and useful in their studies. I am enormously grateful for the incredible support of Hasok Chang and his wonderful group of graduate students, who read the whole draft and discussed it with me in their reading group. Special thanks are due to Céline Henne, Hannah Tomczyk and Bobby Vos, who offered feedback on the entire first draft. I am also most grateful to David Stump, who not only carefully read the entire draft and offered encour-aging comments, but has for years been a wonderful mentor and influenced so much of my work. Many thanks are also due to Jacob Stegenga and the two anonymous referees for Cambridge University Press for offering such positive and constructive feedback.

This work was written during most challenging times when we all were facing a lot of uncertainties during a global pandemic. I had to be very creative with my time and write in the short spells around my daughter's naps, late in to the night and around playtimes while we were in lockdown. I am grateful to my partner, Matt, for sacrificing a lot of sleep to support me in completing this project. I am most grateful to our wonderful daughter, Cailyn, for keeping me grounded and entertained, and for gifting me the privilege of being her mama.

Cambridge Elements ⲥ

Philosophy of Science

Jacob Stegenga
University of Cambridge
Jacob Stegenga is a Reader in the Department of History and Philosophy of Science at the University of Cambridge. He has published widely on fundamental topics in reasoning and rationality and philosophical problems in medicine and biology. Prior to joining Cambridge he taught in the United States and Canada, and he received his PhD from the University of California San Diego.

About the Series
This series of Elements in Philosophy of Science provides an extensive overview of the themes, topics and debates which constitute the philosophy of science. Distinguished specialists provide an up-to-date summary of the results of current research on their topics, as well as offering their own take on those topics and drawing original conclusions.

Cambridge Elements $\equiv$

Philosophy of Science

Printed in the United States
by Baker & Taylor Publisher Services